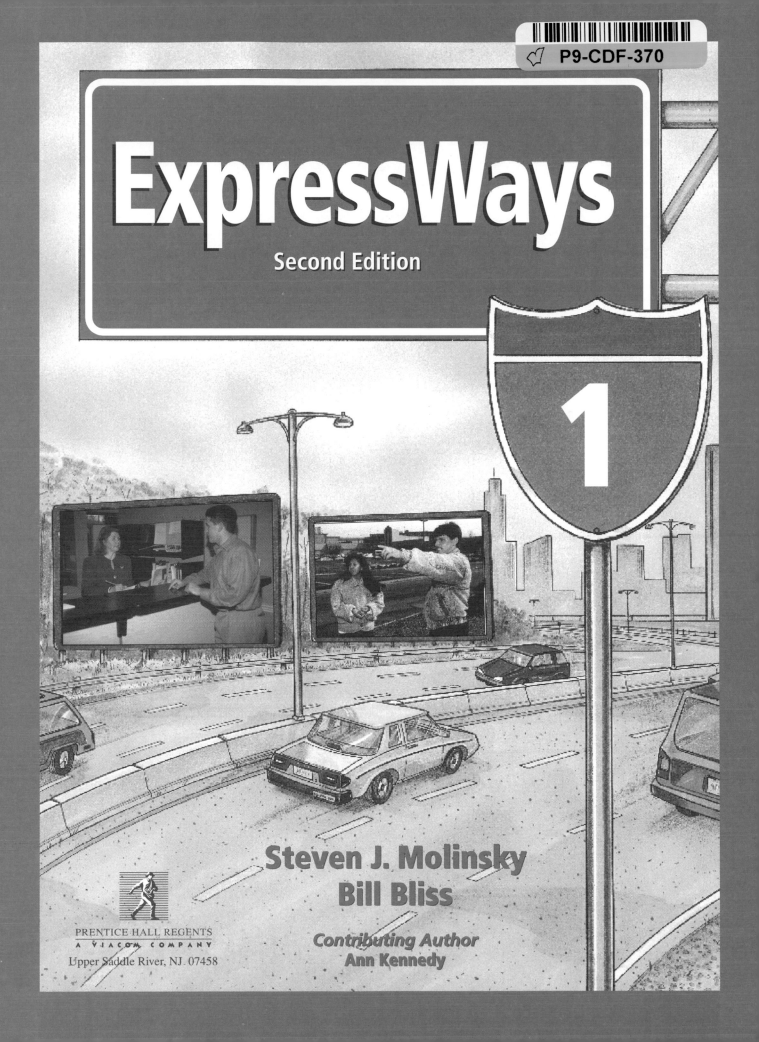

ExpressWays

Second Edition

1

Steven J. Molinsky
Bill Bliss

PRENTICE HALL REGENTS
A VIACOM COMPANY
Upper Saddle River, NJ. 07458

Contributing Author
Ann Kennedy

Molinsky, Steven J.
    ExpressWays 1 / Steven J. Molinsky, Bill Bliss. – – 2nd ed.
      p.   cm.
    Includes index.
    ISBN 0-13-385295-4. (soft cover: alk. paper)
    1. English language– –Textbooks for foreign speakers.   I. Bliss,
Bill. II. Title..
PE1128.M6753   1995
428.2'4– –dc20   95-44120
                                            CIP

Publisher: *Tina Carver*
Director of Production: *Aliza Greenblatt*
Editorial Production/Design Manager: *Dominick Mosco*
Production Supervision/Compositor: *Janice Sivertsen*
Production Editors/Compositors: *Don Kilcoyne/Ken Liao/Christine Mann*
Editorial Supervision: *Janet Johnston*
Production Assistant: *Dana Tamaraz*
Manufacturing Manager: *Ray Keating*

Electronic Art Production Supervision: *Todd Ware*
Electronic Art Production/Scanning: *Marita Froimson*
Electronic Art: *Marita Froimson/Don Kilcoyne/Jan Sivertsen/Ken Liao*
Art Director: *Merle Krumper*
Interior Design: *PC&F and Wanda España*
Photographer: *Paul Tañedo*

Illustrator: *Richard Hill*

© 1996 by PRENTICE HALL REGENTS
Prentice-Hall, Inc.
A Simon & Schuster Company
Upper Saddle River, New Jersey 07458

PRENTICE HALL REGENTS
A VIACOM COMPANY

10   9   8   7   6

ISBN 0-13-385295-4

Prentice-Hall International (UK) Limited, *London*
Prentice-Hall of Australia Pty. Limited, *Sydney*
Prentice-Hall Canada Inc., *Toronto*
Prentice-Hall Hispanoamericana, S.A., *Mexico*
Prentice-Hall of India Private Limited, *New Delhi*
Prentice-Hall of Japan, Inc., *Tokyo*
Simon & Schuster Asia Pte. Ltd., *Singapore*
Editora Prentice-Hall do Brasil, Ltda., *Rio de Janeiro*

EXPRESSWAYS 1 TRAVEL GUIDE

iii

EXIT 5 • At Work   73

APPENDIX   155

ExpressWays is a comprehensive 4-level course for learners of English. Its innovative spiraled curriculum integrates lifeskill topics, functions, and grammar in an imaginative highway theme that puts students *in the fast lane* for an exciting and motivating journey to English language proficiency.

The program consists of the following components:

- **Student Texts** — offering speaking, reading, writing, and listening comprehension practice that integrates grammar and functions in a topic-based curriculum.

- **Activity Workbooks** — offering reinforcement through grammar, reading, writing, and listening comprehension practice fully coordinated with the student texts. The activity workbooks also feature dynamic exercises in pronunciation, rhythm, stress, and intonation.

- *Navigator* **Companion Books** — visually exciting "magazine-style" texts, offering a complete lifeskill curriculum fully integrated with the *ExpressWays* student texts.

- **Teacher's Guides** — providing background notes and expansion activities for all lessons and step-by-step instructions for teachers.

- **Audio Program** — offering realistic presentations of conversations, listening comprehension exercises, and readings from the student texts and workbooks.

- **Picture Program** — featuring Picture Cards for vocabulary development, enrichment exercises, and role playing activities.

- **Placement and Achievement Testing Program** — providing tools for the evaluation of student levels and progress.

The *ExpressWays* series is organized by a spiraled curriculum that is covered at different degrees of intensity and depth at each level. *ExpressWays* 1 and 2 provide beginning-level students with the most important vocabulary, grammar, and functional expressions needed to communicate at a basic level in a full range of situations and contexts. *ExpressWays* 3 and 4 cover the same full range of situations and contexts, but offer intermediate-level students expanded vocabulary, more complex grammar, and a wider choice of functional expressions.

The Dimensions of Communication: Function, Form, and Content

ExpressWays provides dynamic, communicative practice that involves students in lively interactions based on the content of real-life contexts and situations. Every lesson offers students simultaneous practice with one or more functions, the grammatical forms needed to express those functions competently, and the contexts and situations in which the functions and grammar are used. This "tri-dimensional" clustering of function, form, and content is the organizing principle behind each lesson and the cornerstone of the *ExpressWays* approach to functional syllabus design.

ExpressWays offers students broad exposure to uses of language in a variety of relevant contexts: in community, school, employment, home, and social settings. The series gives students practice using a variety of registers, from the formal language someone might use in a job interview, with a customer, or when speaking to an authority figure, to the informal language someone would use when talking with family members, co-workers, or friends.

A special feature of the course is the treatment of discourse strategies — initiating conversations and topics, hesitating, asking for clarification, and other conversation skills.

An Overview

Chapter-Opening Photos

Each chapter-opening page features two photographs of situations that depict key topics presented in the chapter. Students make predictions about who the people are and what they might be saying to each other. In this way, students have the opportunity to share what they already know and to relate the chapter's content to their own lives and experiences.

Guided Conversations

Guided conversations are the dialogs and exercises that are the central learning devices in *ExpressWays*. Each lesson begins with a model conversation that depicts a real-life situation and the vocabulary, grammar, and functions used in the communication exchange. In the exercises that follow, students create new conversations by placing new content into the framework of the model.

Original Student Conversations

Each lesson ends with an open-ended exercise that offers students the opportunity to create and present original conversations based on the theme of the lesson. Students contribute content based on their experiences, ideas, and imaginations.

Follow-Up Exercises and Activities

A variety of follow-up exercises and activities reinforce and build upon the topics, functions, and grammar presented in the guided conversation lessons.

- **Constructions Ahead!** exercises provide focused practice with grammar structures.

- **CrossTalk** activities provide opportunities for students to relate lesson content to their own lives.

- **InterActions** activities provide opportunities for role playing and cooperative learning.

- **Interview** activities encourage students to interview each other as well as people in the community.

- **Community Connections** activities provide task-based homework for students to get out into their communities to practice their language skills.

- **Cultural Intersections** activities offer rich opportunities for cross-cultural comparison.

- **Figure It Out!** activities offer opportunities for problem-solving.

- **Your Turn** activities provide opportunities for writing and discussion of issues presented in the chapter.

- **Listening Exercises** give students intensive listening practice that focuses on functional communication.

- **Reflections** activities provide frequent opportunities for self-assessment, critical thinking, and problem-solving.

- **Reading** passages in every chapter are designed to provide interesting and stimulating content for class discussion. These selections are also available on the accompanying audiotapes for additional listening comprehension practice.

InterChange

This end-of-chapter activity offers students the opportunity to create and present "guided role plays." Each activity consists of a model that students can practice and then use as a basis for their original presentations. Students should be encouraged to be inventive and to use new vocabulary in these presentations and should feel free to adapt and expand the model any way they wish.

Rest Stop

These "free role plays" appear after every few chapters, offering review and synthesis of the topics, functions, and grammar of the preceding chapters. Students are presented with eight scenes depicting conversations between people in various situations. The students determine who the people are and what they are talking about, and then improvise based on their perceptions of the scenes' characters, contexts, and situations. These improvisations promote students' absorption of the preceding chapters' functions and grammar into their repertoire of active language use.

Support and Reference Sections

End-of-Chapter Summaries include the following:

- **Looking Back** — a listing of key vocabulary in the chapter for review.

- **Construction Sign** — a listing of the key grammar structures presented in the chapter.

- **ExpressWays Checklist** — a self-assessment listing of key lifeskills presented in the chapter.

An **Appendix** provides charts of the grammar constructions presented in each chapter, along with a list of cardinal numbers, ordinal numbers, and irregular verbs.

An **Index** provides a convenient reference for locating topics and grammar in the text.

Suggested Teaching Strategies

We encourage you, in using *ExpressWays*, to develop approaches and strategies that are compatible with your own teaching syle and the needs and abilities of your students. While the program does not require any specific method or technique in order to be used effectively, you may find it helpful to review and try out some of the following suggestions. (Specific step-by-step instructions may be found in the *ExpressWays* Teacher's Guides.)

Chapter-Opening Photos

Have students talk about the people and the situations and, as a class or in pairs, predict what the characters might be saying to each other. Students in pairs or small groups may enjoy practicing role plays based on these scenes and then presenting them to the class.

Guided Conversations

1. SETTING THE SCENE: Have students look at the model illustration in the book. Set the scene: Who are the people? What is the situation?

2. LISTENING: With books closed, have students listen to the model conversation — presented by you, by a pair of students, or on the audiotape.

3. CLASS PRACTICE: With books still closed, model each line and have the whole class practice in unison.

4. READING: With books open, have students follow along as two students present the model.

5. PAIR PRACTICE: In pairs, have students practice the model conversation.

6. EXERCISE PRACTICE: (optional) Have pairs of students simultaneously practice all the exercises.

7. EXERCISE PRESENTATIONS: Call on pairs of students to present the exercises.

Original Student Conversations

In these activities, which follow the guided conversations at the end of each lesson, have students create and present original conversations based on the theme of the lesson. Encourage students to be inventive as they create their characters and situations. (You may ask students to prepare their original conversations as homework, then practice them the next day with another student and present them to the class. In this way, students can review the previous day's lesson without actually having to repeat the specific exercises already covered.)

CrossTalk

Have students first work in pairs and then share with the class what they talked about.

InterActions

Have pairs of students practice role playing the activity and then present their role plays to the class.

InterView

Have students circulate around the room to conduct their interviews, or have students interview people outside the class. Students should then report to the class about their interviews.

Community Connections

Have students do the activity individually, in pairs, or in small groups and then report to the class.

Cultural Intersections

Have students do the activity as a class, in pairs, or in small groups.

Reflections

Have students discuss the questions in pairs or small groups, and then share their ideas with the class.

Your Turn

This activity is designed for both writing practice and discussion. Have students discuss the activity as a class, in pairs, or in small groups. Then have students write their responses at home, share their written work with other students, and discuss in class. Students may enjoy keeping a journal of their written work. If time permits, you may want to write a response to each student's journal, sharing your own opinions and experiences as well as reacting to what the student has written. If you are keeping portfolios of students' work, these compositions serve as excellent examples of students' progress in learning English.

Reading

Have students discuss the topic of the reading beforehand, using the pre-reading questions suggested in the Teacher's Guide. Have students then read the passage silently, or have them listen to the passage and take notes as you read it or play the audiotape.

InterChange

Have students practice the model, using the same steps listed above for guided conversations. Then have pairs of students create and present original conversations, using the model dialog as a guide. Encourage students to be inventive and to use new vocabulary. (You may want to assign this exercise as homework, having students prepare their conversations, practice them the next day with another student, and then present them to the class.) Students should present their conversations without referring to the written text, but they should also not memorize them. Rather, they should feel free to adapt and expand them any way they wish.

Rest Stop

Have students talk about the people and the situations, and then present role plays based on the scenes. Students may refer back to previous lessons as a resource, but they should not simply re-use specific conversations. (You may want to assign these exercises as written homework, having students prepare their conversations, practice them the next day with another student, and then present them to the class.)

We hope that *ExpressWays* offers you and your students a journey to English that is meaningful, effective, and entertaining. Have a nice trip!

Steven J. Molinsky
Bill Bliss

ExpressWays

Second Edition

1

MEETING AND GREETING PEOPLE

Take Exit 1 to . . .

- ↗ Greet someone and introduce yourself
- ↗ Introduce members of your family
- ↗ Give your name and tell how to spell it
- ↗ Give your address and telephone number
- ↗ Tell where you're from
- ↗ Exchange information, using *to be, yes/no questions,* and *wh-questions*

Functions This Exit!

Greeting People

Introductions

Asking for and Reporting Information

Roger and Carol are meeting for the first time. What do you think they're saying to each other?

Nancy is filling out a form and is asking Edward for some information. What do you think they're saying to each other?

Carlos

Kim

A. Hello. My name is Carlos.

B. Hi. I'm Kim. Nice to meet you.

A. Nice meeting you, too.

1 Doris · · · · Jane

2 Tom · · · · Karen

3 Mary · · · · Bob
Warner · · · Wilson

4 Richard · · · Steve
Simon · · · Smith

5 Brian · · · · Jessica

**Introduce yourself
to another student
in your English
class.**

2

ExpressWays

meet	Hello	is	you
name	meeting	My	I'm

1.
_____Hello_____. My name is Tom.

Hi. My _____ is Bill.

2.
_____. I'm Sally.

_____ name is Gloria. Nice to meet _____.

3.
Hello. My name _____ Peter.

Hello. _____ Bob.

4.
Hi. _____ name is Jennifer.

Hi. I'm Steve. Nice to _____ you.

5.
_____. My _____ _____ Margaret.

Hi. _____ Mary. Nice to _____ _____.

6.
_____. _____ Richard. Nice to _____ _____.

Nice _____ _____, too.

InterActions

These people are meeting each other. What do you think they're saying?

1.

2.

3

my husband, Michael

A. Hi! How are you?

B. Fine. And you?

A. Fine, thanks. I'd like to introduce you to my husband, Michael.

B. Nice to meet you.

1 my wife, Barbara

2 my father, Mr. Peterson

3 my mother, Mrs. Chen

4 my brother, George

5 my sister, Irene

Introduce a friend to somebody else.

ExpressWays

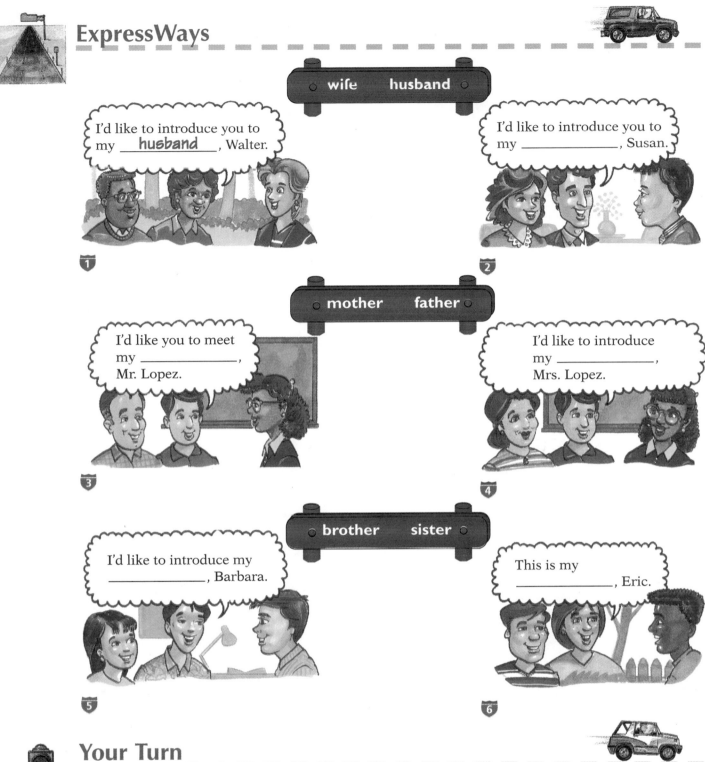

wife   husband

I'd like to introduce you to my _____husband_____, Walter.

1

I'd like to introduce you to my _____, Susan.

2

mother   father

I'd like you to meet my _____, Mr. Lopez.

3

I'd like to introduce my _____, Mrs. Lopez.

4

brother   sister

I'd like to introduce my _____, Barbara.

5

This is my _____, Eric.

6

Your Turn

Now introduce members of YOUR family. Bring in photographs of family members and introduce your family to the class.

I'd like to introduce you to my grandmother. Her name is Sarah.

I'd like you to meet my husband, Tung.

This is my sister. Her name is Margarita.

5

Maria Sanchez

A. What's your last name?

B. Sanchez.

A. Could you spell that, please?

B. S-A-N-C-H-E-Z.

A. And your first name?

B. Maria.

1 John Clayton

2 Nancy Brenner

3 Linda Kwan

4 Robert Kelton

5 Lefty Grimes

Ask another person's name and how to spell it.

A B C D E F G H I J K L M N O P Q R S T U V W X Y Z
a b c d e f g h i j k l m n o p q r s t u v w x y z

Listen 1

Listen and write the missing letters.

1. B _r_ enner
2. Barb___ra
3. C___ayton
4. S___ith
5. K___ ___n

6. ___ ___l ___on
7. ___ ___ ___ ___rson
8. M___ ___h ___ ___l
9. h___ ___ ___ ___nd
10. ___ ___ ___ ___ ___ ___ ___

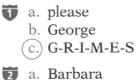

Listen 2

Listen and choose the right answer.

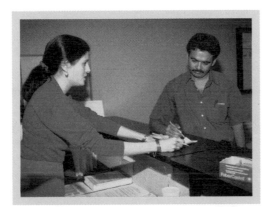

1. a. please
   b. George
   c. G-R-I-M-E-S

2. a. Barbara
   b. brother
   c. first

3. a. husband
   b. Robert
   c. name

4. a. last namc
   b. Sanchez
   c. And you?

5. a. Mrs. Chen
   b. Linda
   c. Hello

6. a. Clayton
   b. last name
   c. K-E-L-T-O-N

Fill It In!

Fill in the missing
letters in the movie sign.

Westown Mall Cinema

1 MY _AME I_ MICHAEL
2 MY BROT_ER BOB
3 MY S_STER NANCY
4 __EASE !
5 MY __THER & F__HER

10 Main Street
423-6978

A. What's your address?

B. 10 Main Street.

A. And your telephone number?

B. 423-6978.

1 5 Summer Street
531-7624

2 7 Pond Road
899-3263

3 14 Maple Avenue
475-1182

4 19 Howard Road
542-7306*

5 1813† Central Avenue
733-8920

Find out another person's address and telephone number.

* 0 = "oh"
† 1813 = eighteen thirteen

I 2 3•4 5 6 7 8 9 10 II 12 13 14 15 16 17 18•19 20

Listen 1

Listen and write the number of the address you hear.

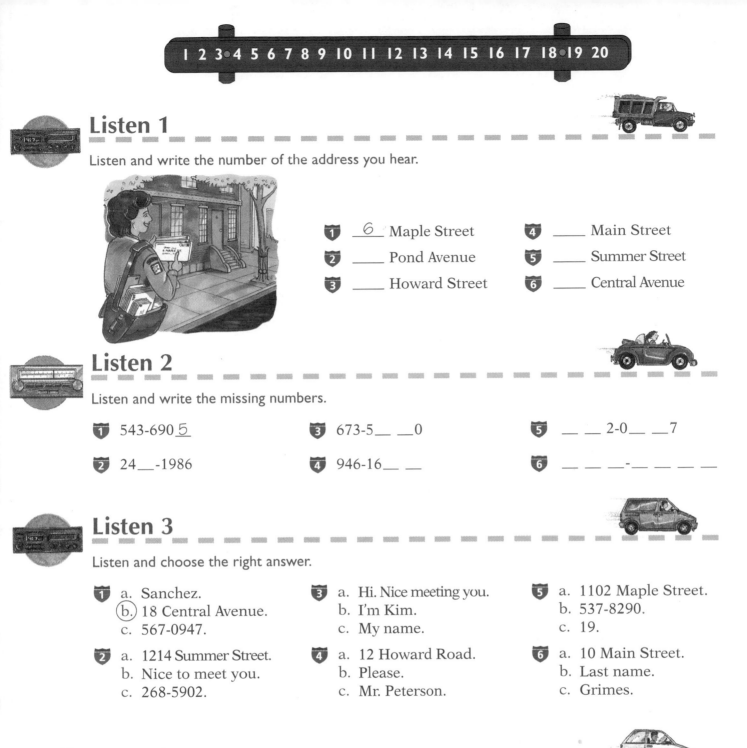

1. __6__ Maple Street
2. ____ Pond Avenue
3. ____ Howard Street
4. ____ Main Street
5. ____ Summer Street
6. ____ Central Avenue

Listen 2

Listen and write the missing numbers.

1. 543-690 _5_

2. 24__-1986

3. 673-5__ __0

4. 946-16__ __

5. __ __ 2-0__ __7

6. __ __ __-__ __ __ __

Listen 3

Listen and choose the right answer.

1. a. Sanchez.
   b. 18 Central Avenue.
   c. 567-0947.

2. a. 1214 Summer Street.
   b. Nice to meet you.
   c. 268-5902.

3. a. Hi. Nice meeting you.
   b. I'm Kim.
   c. My name.

4. a. 12 Howard Road.
   b. Please.
   c. Mr. Peterson.

5. a. 1102 Maple Street.
   b. 537-8290.
   c. 19.

6. a. 10 Main Street.
   b. Last name.
   c. Grimes.

InterView

Interview another student in your class and fill out the form below.

Name _____
     First   M.I.   Last

Address _____
        Number   Street

Telephone Number _____ - _____

9

A. What's your name?

B. Kenji.

A. Where are you from?

B. Japan.

A. Oh. Are you from Tokyo?

B. No. I'm from Osaka.

1 Maria
Italy

2 Hector
Mexico

3 Mohammed
Egypt

4 Anna
Russia

5 Mei Ling
China

You're meeting someone at a party. What's the person's name, and where is that person from?

ExpressWays

I   My

1 ___I___ 'm from San Francisco.

_____ name is Michael.

She   Her

2 _____ name is Anna.

_____ is from Italy.

We   Our

3 _____ are Miguel and Maria.

_____ father is Mr. Sanchez.

He   His

4 _____ name is Takashi.

_____ 's from Kyoto.

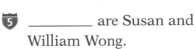

They   Their

5 _____ are Susan and William Wong.

_____ address is 15 Howard Street.

You   Your

6 _____ are Mrs. Baxter.

_____ first name is Doris.

What's the Question?

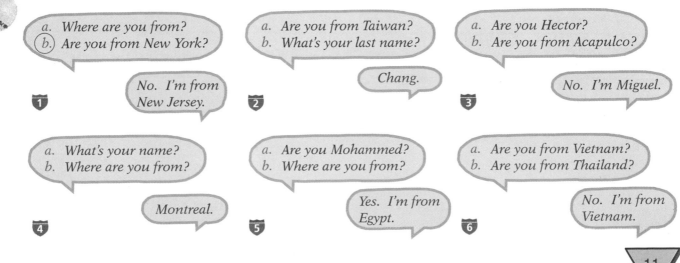

1
a. Where are you from?
b. Are you from New York?

No. I'm from New Jersey.

2
a. Are you from Taiwan?
b. What's your last name?

Chang.

3
a. Are you Hector?
b. Are you from Acapulco?

No. I'm Miguel.

4
a. What's your name?
b. Where are you from?

Montreal.

5
a. Are you Mohammed?
b. Where are you from?

Yes. I'm from Egypt.

6
a. Are you from Vietnam?
b. Are you from Thailand?

No. I'm from Vietnam.

11

INTERCHANGE

Nice to Meet You

A. Hello. My name is Franco Rossi.

B. Hello. I'm Harry Miller.

A. Are you American?

B. Yes, I am. I'm from New York. How about you?

A. I'm Italian. I'm from Rome.

B. Nice to meet you.

A. Nice meeting you, too.

Franco Rossi	Harry Miller
Italian	American
Rome	New York

1 Carol Williams   Carmen Lopez
Canadian   Mexican
Toronto   Mexico City

2 Charles Whitmore   Ali Hassan
British   Egyptian
London   Cairo

3 David Clarke   Asako Tanaka
Australian   Japanese
Melbourne   Tokyo

4 Rick Starlight   Natasha Markova
American   Russian
Hollywood   Moscow

You're an airplane passenger on an international flight. Create an original conversation, using the model dialog above as a guide. Feel free to adapt and expand the model any way you wish.

ExpressWays

| he | she | they | you | is |
| his | her | their | your | are |

1 What's __your__ name?   Miguel.

Where _____ you from?   Mexico.

2 Where _____ _____ from?   He's from Korea.

What's _____ name?   Kim.

3 _____ _____ from Canada?   Yes, she is.

_____ _____ name Janet?   No. Her name is Julie.

4 _____ _____ from China?   Yes, they are.

What _____ _____ last name?   Chen.

Listen

Listen and choose the best answer.

1
  a. Yes, I am.
  b. 10 Main Street.
  c. I'm from Washington.

2
  a. You are.
  b. Yes, I am.
  c. Hello. I'm Harry.

3
  a. No.
  b. How about you?
  c. N-E-W Y-O-R-K.

4
  a. N-U-M-B-E-R.
  b. 768-5520.
  c. And you?

5
  a. 389.
  b. N-A-M-E.
  c. I'm Richard.

6
  a. How about you?
  b. Yes, I am.
  c. I'm from Japan.

13

Reading: *Meet These People*

Antonio is a student in the United States. He's Italian. He's from Venice. His wife is French. Her name is Nicole. She's from Paris. Their last name is DiMarco. Their address is 190 Harrison Avenue in San Francisco, California.

Maria is from Bogota. She's Colombian. Soo Jung is Korean. She's from Seoul. Maria and Soo Jung are students at the Adult Education Center. The address of their school is 1200 Broad Street in Fairfax, Virginia.

Meet Brian Wheeler. He's from Chicago. He's a student at Lakeville High School. His address is 1994 Westville Avenue in Chicago. His telephone number is 792-4380.

What's the Answer?

1 Antonio is _____.
   a. from the United States
   b. Italian
   c. French

2 Nicole's last name is _____.
   a. Harrison
   b. French
   c. DiMarco

3 Maria is _____.
   a. in Bogota
   b. Korean
   c. Colombian

4 Soo Jung's _____ is on Broad Street.
   a. student
   b. school
   c. Virginia

5 Maria and Soo Jung are _____.
   a. from Seoul
   b. students
   c. Colombian

6 Brian is a student at _____.
   a. Chicago
   b. Wheeler
   c. Lakeville High School

7 His _____ number is 792-4380.
   a. telephone
   b. address
   c. student

8 Brian's last name is _____.
   a. Westville
   b. Wheeler
   c. Chicago

Constructions Ahead!

I'm	my
he's	his
she's	her
we're	our
you're	your
they're	their

1 He's from El Salvador. ___His___ name is Miguel.

2 _____ last name is Kwan. They're from Bejing.

3 _____ from Russia. Her mother is Russian.

4 We're from Spain. _____ family is from Madrid.

5 _____ American. I'm from Miami.

6 You're Mrs. Waterson. What's _____ first name, please?

7 I'm Swedish. _____ last name is Nilsen.

8 They're Australian. _____ from Melbourne.

9 _____ Charles. His wife's name is Nancy.

10 Our last name is Rodriguez. _____ from Puerto Rico.

11 _____ Brazilian. I'm from Rio.

12 Is _____ last name Robertson? Are you from Dallas? _____ last name is Robertson. And I'm from Dallas, too.

InterView

Interview your classmates, your neighbors, or people you work with. Fill out the chart below and report your findings to the class.

| *What's your name?* | *What's your nationality?* | *What country are you from?* | *What city are you from?* |

Name	Nationality	Country	City
. . . .	. . . .	. . . .	. . . .
. . . .	. . . .	. . . .	. . . .
. . . .	. . . .	. . . .	. . . .
. . . .	. . . .	. . . .	. . . .
. . . .	. . . .	. . . .	. . . .

Looking Back

☐ **Personal Information**
name
last name
first name
address
street
road
avenue
telephone
number

☐ **Family Members**
husband
wife
father
mother
brother
sister

☐ **Countries**
China
Egypt
Italy

Japan
Mexico
Russia

☐ **Nationalities**
American
Australian
British
Canadian
Egyptian
Italian

Japanese
Mexican
Russian

☐ **Cardinal Numbers: 1–19**
1 one
2 two
3 three
4 four
5 five
6 six
7 seven

8 eight
9 nine
10 ten
11 eleven
12 twelve
13 thirteen
14 fourteen
15 fifteen
16 sixteen
17 seventeen
18 eighteen
19 nineteen

Now Leaving Exit 1 Construction Area

☐ **To Be**
☐ **To Be: Yes/No Questions**
☐ **Subject Pronouns**
☐ **Possessive Adjectives**
☐ **WH-Questions**

Sorry for the inconvenience. For more information see page 157.

ExpressWays Checklist

I can . . .
☐ greet someone and introduce myself
☐ introduce members of my family
☐ give my name and tell how to spell it
☐ give my address and telephone number
☐ tell where I'm from

16

Exit 2

PEOPLE AND PLACES

Take Exit 2 to . . .

➔ Call directory assistance, using *wh-questions*

➔ Make telephone calls, using *to be*

➔ Discover various places in the community

➔ Tell about everyday activities, using the present continuous tense

Functions This Exit!

Asking for and Reporting Information
Greeting People
Identifying
Leave Taking

Hector is calling the directory assistance operator. What do you think they're saying to each other?

Two friends are going to different places, and they meet on the street. What do you think they're saying to each other?

863-4227

A. Directory assistance. What city?

B. Chicago. I'd like the number of Mary Nielson.

A. How do you spell that?

B. N-I-E-L-S-O-N.

A. What street?

B. Hudson Avenue.

A. Just a moment . . . The number is 863-4227.

1 968-3135

2 747-6360

3 237-8044

4 328-1191

5 623-7575

Call directory assistance!

Matching Lines

_b_ **1** I'd like the number of ____.   a. 423-7771.

____ **2** What street?   b. Sally Craven.

____ **3** The number is ____.   c. Miami.

____ **4** What city?   d. C-R-A-V-E-N.

____ **5** How do you spell that?   e. Harbor Drive.

Listen 1

Listen and choose the answer to the question you hear.

1 547-2055 ☑ Yes   **4** 356-9473 ☐ Yes
                ☐ No   ☐ No

2 498-5930 ☐ Yes   **5** 285-2841 ☐ Yes
                ☐ No   ☐ No

3 624-6835 ☐ Yes   **6** 777-5962 ☐ Yes
                ☐ No   ☐ No

Listen 2

Listen and write the missing numbers.

1 5 7 3 - 5 1 0 8   **3** ____ - ____   **5** ____ - ____

2 ____ - ____   **4** ____ - ____   **6** ____ - ____

Crossed Lines

Oh, no! There's a problem with the telephone. Put the following lines in the correct order.

____ G-R-E-E-N-L-E-Y.

____ San Diego. I'd like the number of Howard Greenley.

____ Maple Drive.

____ Just a moment. The number is 693-8257.

_1_ Directory assistance. What city?

____ How do you spell that?

____ What street?

REFLECTIONS
What's the number of directory assistance in your city? in another state you know? How much is a call to directory assistance?

Discuss in pairs or small groups, and then share your ideas with the class.

19

A. Hello.

B. Hello, Fred?

A. I'm sorry. You have the wrong number.

B. Is this 328-7178?

A. No, it isn't.

B. Oh. Sorry.

Constructions Ahead!

1. _Are_ you Japanese?
2. _____ she from Cairo?
3. _____ this 832-1924?
4. _____ they from Mexico?
5. _____ he Canadian?
6. _____ your number 349-9654?
7. _____ Mr. and Mrs. Lee from Hawaii?
8. _____ Alan and Bill your brothers?
9. _____ I on Main Street?
10. _____ we on Riverview Drive?

Am	I
Is	{ he she it } here?
Are	{ we you they }

REFLECTIONS
Is your telephone number in the telephone book, or is it unlisted?

Discuss in pairs or small groups, and then share your ideas with the class.

More Constructions Ahead!

No, I'm not.   No, { he she it } isn't.   No, { we you they } aren't.

1. Is your husband American? — No, _he_ _isn't_.

2. Are your neighbors quiet? — No, _____ _____.

3. Is this 435-9002? — No, _____ _____.

4. Are you Mrs. Wells? — No, _____ _____.

5. Is she your wife? — No, _____ _____.

6. Am I on Maple Street? — No, _____ _____.

Mike

A. Hello. This is Mike. Is Peter there?

B. No, he isn't. He's at the supermarket.

A. Oh, I see. I'll call back later. Thank you.

Patty

A. Hello. This is Patty. Is Janet there?

B. No, she isn't. She's at the bank.

A. Oh, I see. I'll call back later. Thank you.

Bobby

A. Hello. This is Bobby. Are Timmy and Billy there?

B. No, they aren't. They're at the library.

A. Oh, I see. I'll call back later. Thank you.

Judy

1

Tim

2

Mrs. Gold

3

Alice

4

George

5

You're calling somebody, and that person isn't there!

22

People and Places!

am   is   are

1 George ___is___ at the
___supermarket___ .

2 Aki and Tom _____ at the
_____ .

3 Mr. Hernandez _____ at the
_____ .

4 I _____ at the
_____ .

5 My husband and I _____ at the
_____ .

6 You _____ at
_____ .

7 Mrs. Tanaka _____ at the
_____ .

8 Grandpa _____ at the
_____ .

23

the post office

the library

A. Hi! How are you today?

B. Fine. And you?

A. Fine, thanks. Where are you going?

B. To the library. How about you?

A. I'm going to the post office.

B. Well, nice seeing you.

A. Nice seeing you, too.

the clinic *the bank* *school* *the supermarket* *the museum* *the park*

1   2   3

the mall *the movies* *the airport* *the zoo*

Say hello to a friend you meet on the street!

4   5

Where Is Everybody Going?

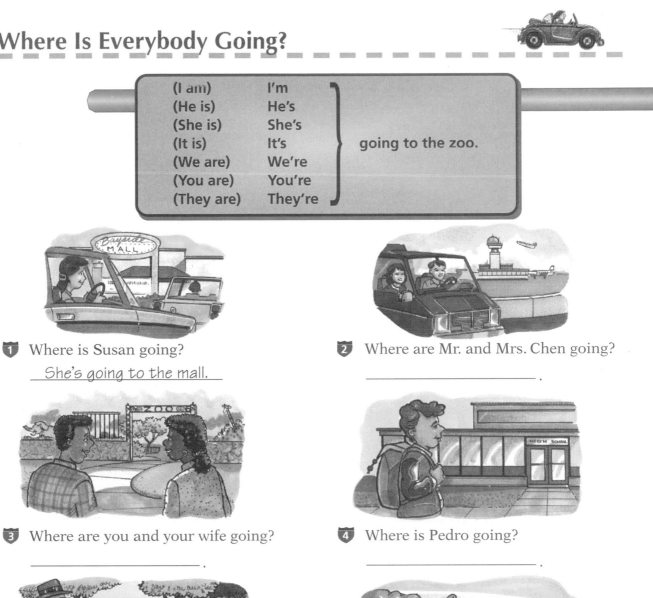

(I am)	I'm
(He is)	He's
(She is)	She's
(It is)	It's · going to the zoo.
(We are)	We're
(You are)	You're
(They are)	They're

1 Where is Susan going?

She's going to the mall.

2 Where are Mr. and Mrs. Chen going?

_____ .

3 Where are you and your wife going?

_____ .

4 Where is Pedro going?

_____ .

 5 Where are you going?

_____ .

6 Where is the train going?

_____ .

Figure It Out!

Bring a "prop" to class—for example, a letter, a book, or a briefcase. Other students in the class then guess where you're going.

You're going to the post office.

You're going to the library.

You're going to work.

A. What are you doing?
B. I'm fixing my car.

A. What's Linda doing?
B. She's studying.

A. What's John doing?
B. He's cleaning the garage.

A. What are you doing?
B. We're doing our homework.

1 Richard
fixing his bicycle

2 you
making breakfast

3 Jennifer and Melissa
cleaning their room

4 Kevin
dancing

5 Miss Henderson
looking for her contact lens

What's everybody doing? Ask about students in your class.

Constructions Ahead!

(I am)	I'm
(He is)	He's
(She is)	She's
(It is)	It's
(We are)	We're
(You are)	You're
(They are)	They're

} working.

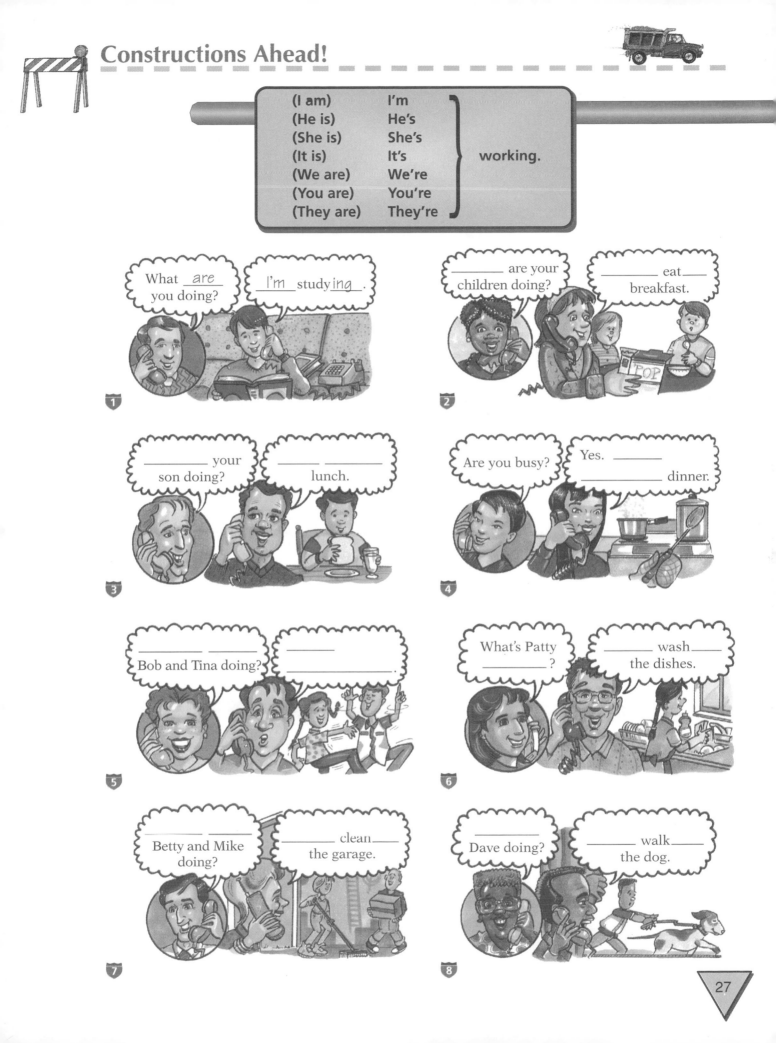

1
What _are_ you doing?
___I'm___ study_ing_.

2
_____ are your children doing?
_____ eat____ breakfast.

3
_____ your son doing?
_____ _____ lunch.

4
Are you busy?
Yes. _____ _____ dinner.

5
_____ _____ Bob and Tina doing?
_____ _____.

6
What's Patty _____?
_____ wash____ the dishes.

7
_____ _____ Betty and Mike doing?
_____ clean____ the garage.

8
_____ _____ Dave doing?
_____ walk____ the dog.

27

More Constructions Ahead!

(I am)	I'm		my
(He is)	He's		his
(She is)	She's	cleaning	her	room.
(We are)	We're		our
(You are)	You're		your
(They are)	They're		their

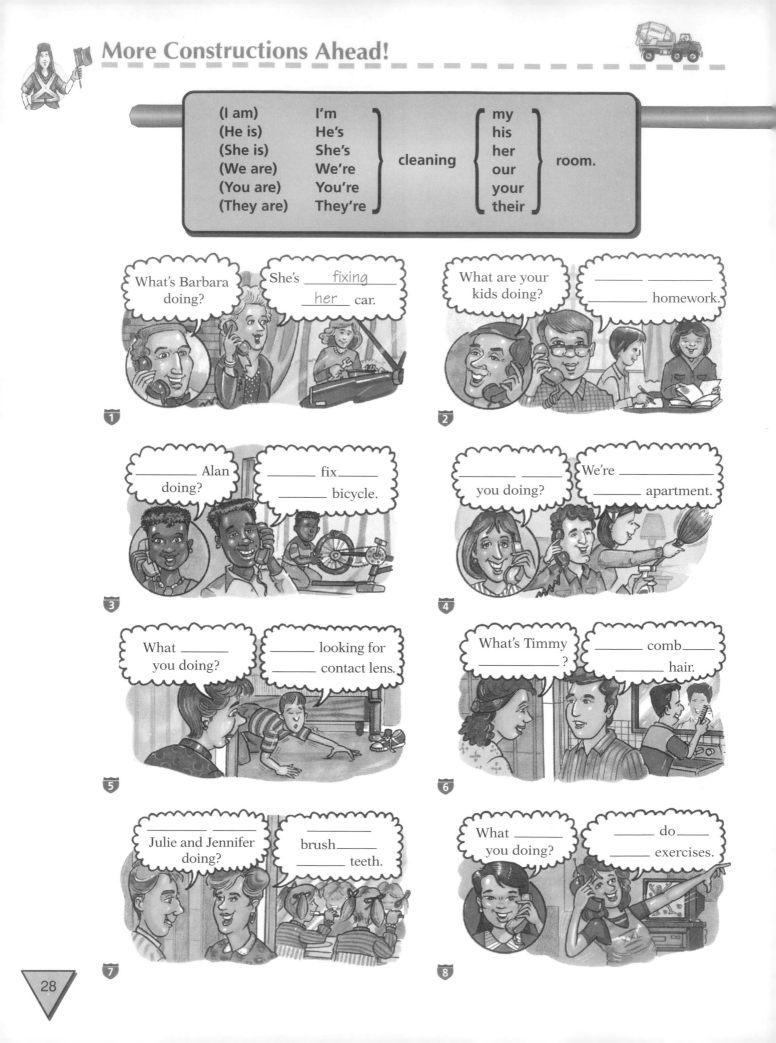

1
What's Barbara doing?
She's ___fixing___ ___her___ car.

2
What are your kids doing?
_____ _____ _____ homework.

3
_____ Alan doing?
_____ fix_____ _____ bicycle.

4
_____ _____ you doing?
We're _____ _____ apartment.

5
What _____ you doing?
_____ looking for _____ contact lens.

6
What's Timmy _____?
_____ comb_____ _____ hair.

7
_____ _____ Julie and Jennifer doing?
brush_____ _____ teeth.

8
What _____ you doing?
_____ do_____ _____ exercises.

Listen

Listen to the conversation and choose the correct picture.

1. ✔ ____

2. ____ ____

3. ____ ____

4. ____ ____

5. ____ ____

6. ____ ____

7. ____ ____

8. ____ ____

9. ____ ____

10. ____ ____

Figure It Out!

Pantomime an action and have others guess what you're doing. For example:

You're walking the dog.   *You're washing the dishes.*   *You're dancing.*

INTERCHANGE

I Can't Talk Right Now. I'm Taking a Shower.

A. Hello, Steve? This is Jackie.

B. Hi. How are you doing?

A. Pretty good. How about you?

B. Okay. Listen, I can't talk right now.
I'm taking a shower.

A. Oh, okay. I'll call back later.

B. Speak to you soon.

A. Good-bye.

Steve

taking a shower

Jeff

Pamela

1 studying

Beth

Debbie

2 eating lunch

Paul

Glen

3 cooking dinner

Gloria

Kathy

4 feeding the baby

A friend is calling you on the telephone, but you can't talk right now. Create an original conversation, using the model dialog above as a guide. Feel free to adapt and expand the model any way you wish.

Reading: *Steve's Friends Can't Talk Right Now*

Steve is calling his friends, but they can't talk right now. His friend Debbie can't talk right now. She's making lunch. His friend Bill can't talk right now. He's cleaning his garage. His friends Carol and Susan can't talk right now. They're doing their homework. His friend Sally is taking a shower, and his friends Paul and John are studying.

Steve can't talk to his friends right now. He'll call back later.

What's the Answer?

1. What's Steve doing?
2. What's Debbie doing?
3. What's Bill doing?

4. What are Carol and Susan doing?
5. What's Sally doing?
6. What are Paul and John doing?

Fill It In!

Fill in the correct answer.

Luis   Debbie   Alex   Carmen   Mrs. Mendoza   Mr. Mendoza

This is the Mendoza family.

Luis Mendoza is _____studying_____ [1].

Debbie is _____ [2]

_____ [3] room. Carmen is _____ [4] lunch.

Alex is _____ [5].

Mr. Mendoza is _____ [6] his car. And Mrs. Mendoza is _____ [7] the sink.

The Mendoza family is very busy today.

Your Turn

For Writing and Discussion
Tell a story about YOUR family.

What's everybody in your family doing today?

Tell your story to the other students in your class. Listen to their stories and find out what people in THEIR families are doing.

Looking Back

☐ **Community**
airport
bank
clinic
laundromat
library
mall
movies (movie theater)
museum
park
post office

school
supermarket
zoo

☐ **Everyday Activities**
brushing (my) teeth
cleaning (my) room
cleaning the garage
combing (my) hair
cooking dinner
doing (my) exercises

doing (my) homework
eating lunch
feeding the baby
fixing (my) bicycle
fixing (my) car
making breakfast
studying
taking a shower
walking the dog
washing the dishes

☐ **Telephone**
directory assistance
number

☐ **Family Members**
baby
parents

Now Leaving Exit 2 Construction Area

☐ **To Be: Yes/No Questions**
☐ **To Be: Negatives**
☐ **Present Continuous Tense**
☐ **Possessive Adjectives**
☐ **WH-Questions**

Sorry for the inconvenience. For more information see page 158.

ExpressWays Checklist

I can . . .

☐ call directory assistance
☐ make telephone calls
☐ identify places in the community
☐ tell about everyday activities

32

Exit 3

GETTING AROUND TOWN

Take Exit 3 to . . .

➤ Describe the locations of places in the community, using *there is*

➤ Access public transportation, using *to be* and the simple present tense

➤ Give directions to places in the community, using imperatives

Functions This Exit!

Directions-Location

Asking for and Reporting Information

Attracting Attention

Gratitude

Checking and Indicating Understanding

Asking for Repetition

Steven is giving directions to someone. What do you think they're saying to each other?

Elena is asking the bus driver a question. What do you think they're saying to each other?

A. Excuse me. Is there a post office nearby?

B. Yes. There's a post office on Main Street.

A. On Main Street?

B. Yes. It's on Main Street, next to the bank.

A. Thank you.

A. Excuse me. Is there a laundromat nearby?

B. Yes. There's a laundromat on Grand Avenue.

A. On Grand Avenue?

B. Yes. It's on Grand Avenue, across from the bus station.

A. Thanks.

A. Excuse me. Is there a drug store nearby?

B. Yes. There's a drug store on River Street.

A. On River Street?

B. Yes. It's on River Street, between the library and the clinic.

A. Thanks very much.

A. Excuse me. Is there a supermarket nearby?

B. Yes. There's a supermarket on Davis Boulevard.

A. On Davis Boulevard?

B. Yes. It's on Davis Boulevard, around the corner from the movie theater.

A. Thank you very much.

1 hotel?

2 parking lot?

3 grocery store?

4 gas station?

5 park?

6 clinic?

7 bank?

Ask a person on the street if a place is nearby.

Where Are These Places?

next to • on across from around the corner from • between

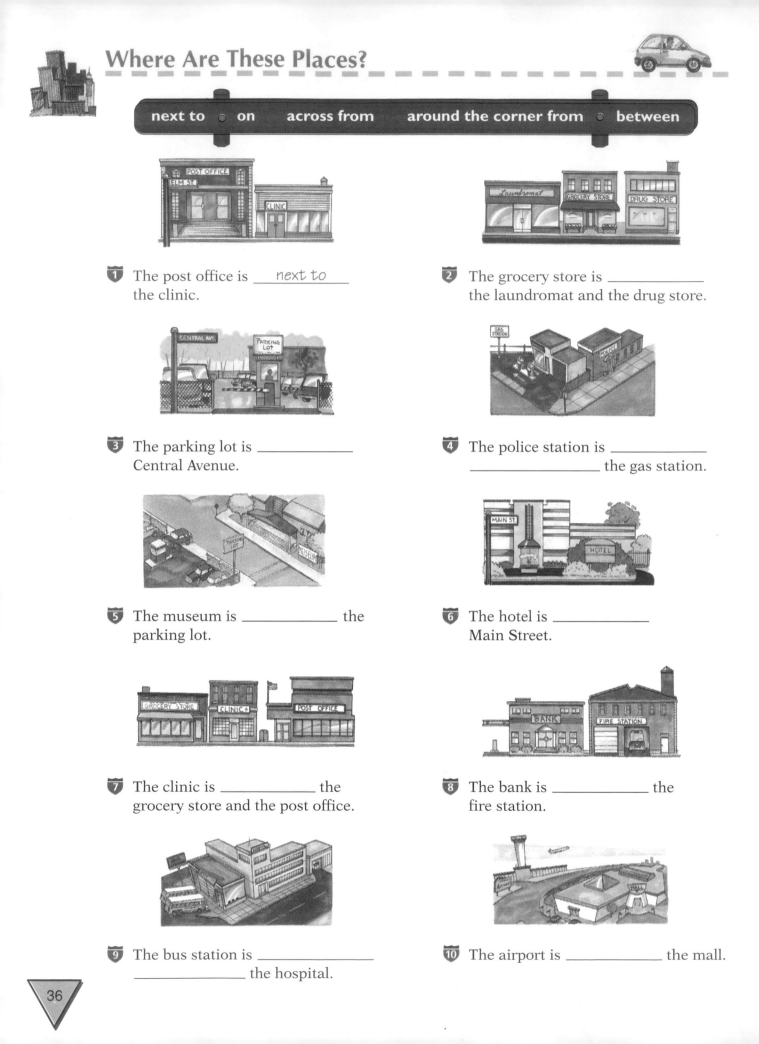

1 The post office is ___next to___ the clinic.

2 The grocery store is _____ the laundromat and the drug store.

3 The parking lot is _____ Central Avenue.

4 The police station is _____ _____ the gas station.

5 The museum is _____ the parking lot.

6 The hotel is _____ Main Street.

7 The clinic is _____ the grocery store and the post office.

8 The bank is _____ the fire station.

9 The bus station is _____ _____ the hospital.

10 The airport is _____ the mall.

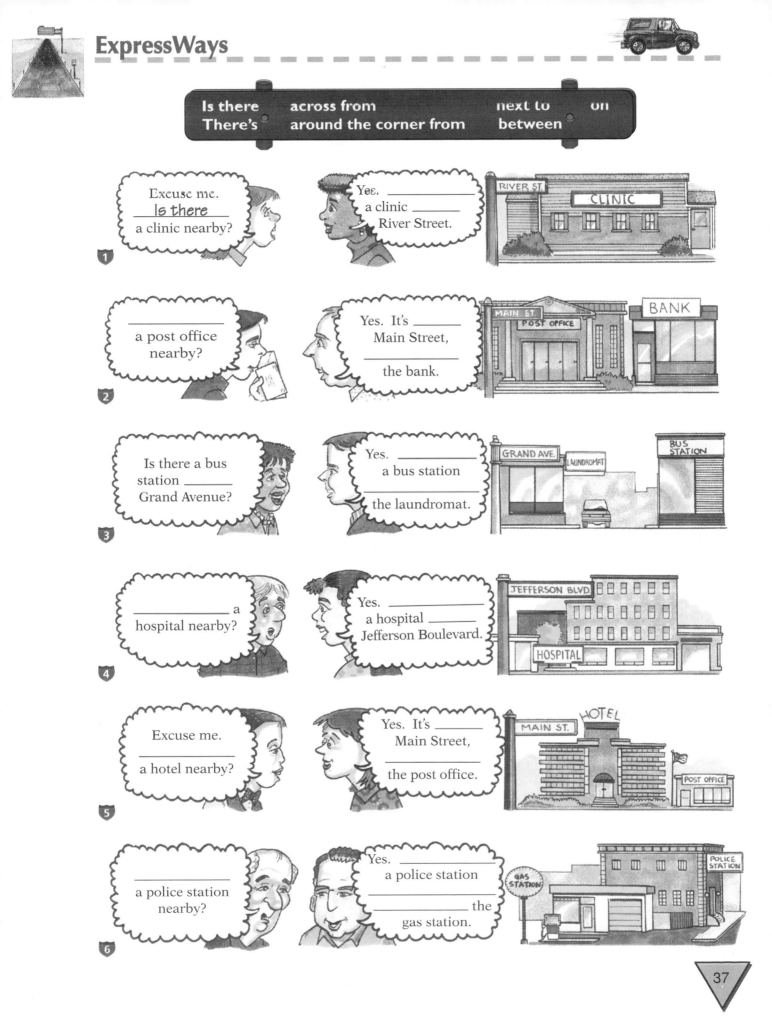

Is there   across from   next to   on
There's   around the corner from   between

1. Excuse me. **Is there** a clinic nearby?

Yes. _____ a clinic _____ River Street.

2. _____ a post office nearby?

Yes. It's _____ Main Street, _____ the bank.

3. Is there a bus station _____ Grand Avenue?

Yes. _____ a bus station _____ the laundromat.

4. _____ a hospital nearby?

Yes. _____ a hospital _____ Jefferson Boulevard.

5. Excuse me. _____ a hotel nearby?

Yes. It's _____ Main Street, _____ the post office.

6. _____ a police station nearby?

Yes. _____ a police station _____ the gas station.

Listen and choose the correct place.

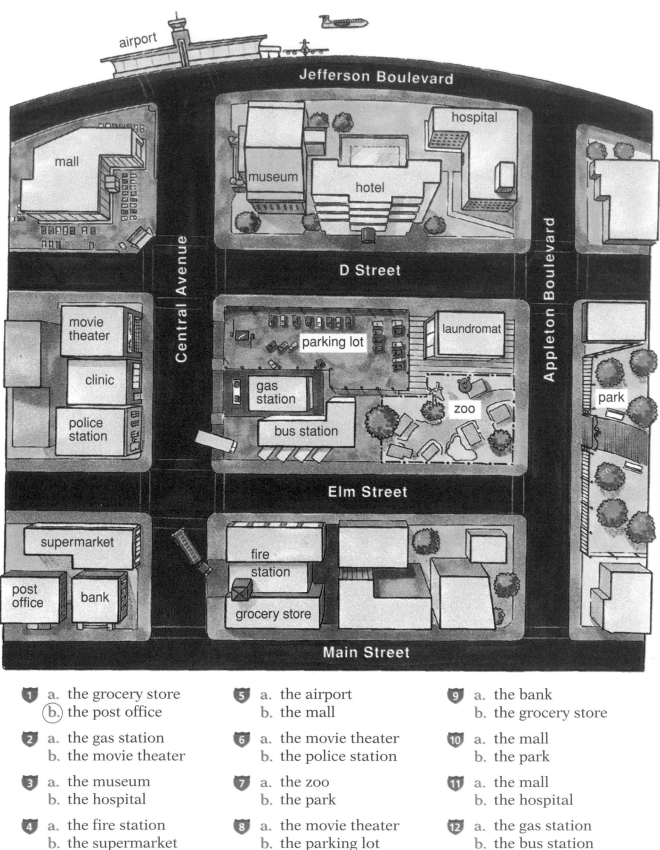

airport

Jefferson Boulevard

mall

hospital

museum

hotel

D Street

Central Avenue

movie theater

laundromat

parking lot

clinic

gas station

zoo

park

Appleton Boulevard

police station

bus station

Elm Street

supermarket

fire station

post office

bank

grocery store

Main Street

1. a. the grocery store
   b. the post office

2. a. the gas station
   b. the movie theater

3. a. the museum
   b. the hospital

4. a. the fire station
   b. the supermarket

5. a. the airport
   b. the mall

6. a. the movie theater
   b. the police station

7. a. the zoo
   b. the park

8. a. the movie theater
   b. the parking lot

9. a. the bank
   b. the grocery store

10. a. the mall
    b. the park

11. a. the mall
    b. the hospital

12. a. the gas station
    b. the bus station

CrossTalk

With a partner, talk about your neighborhoods.

A. Is there a clinic in your neighborhood?
B. Yes, there is.

A. Is there a bank in your neighborhood?
B. No, there isn't.

Then report to the class about each other's neighborhoods.

Your Turn

For Writing and Discussion

My Neighborhood

Draw a map to show the places in your neighborhood. Then tell about the places.

Community Connections

Walk around the neighborhood of your school. Which of the following places are near your school? Where are the places located?

- [ ] a post office _____
- [ ] a laundromat _____
- [ ] a bus station _____
- [ ] a drug store _____
- [ ] a parking lot _____
- [ ] a hotel _____
- [ ] a police station _____
- [ ] a gas station _____

- [ ] a clinic _____
- [ ] a supermarket _____
- [ ] a fire station _____
- [ ] an airport _____
- [ ] a museum _____
- [ ] a grocery store _____
- [ ] a hospital _____
- [ ] a mall _____

to Westville? to Riverside

bus
the Number 30 bus

A. Excuse me. Does this bus go to Westville?

B. No, it doesn't. It goes to Riverside.

A. Oh, I see. Tell me, which bus goes to Westville?

B. The Number 30 bus.

A. Thanks very much.

to Brooklyn? to the Bronx

1 train
the D train

to San Francisco?

to San Diego

2 plane
flight 64

to Washington? to Boston

3 train
the Capitol Express

uptown? downtown

4 bus
Bus Number 27

to the Bahamas?

to Puerto Rico

5 ship
The Sunshine Queen

Ask about a bus,
train, ship, or
plane.

Constructions Ahead!

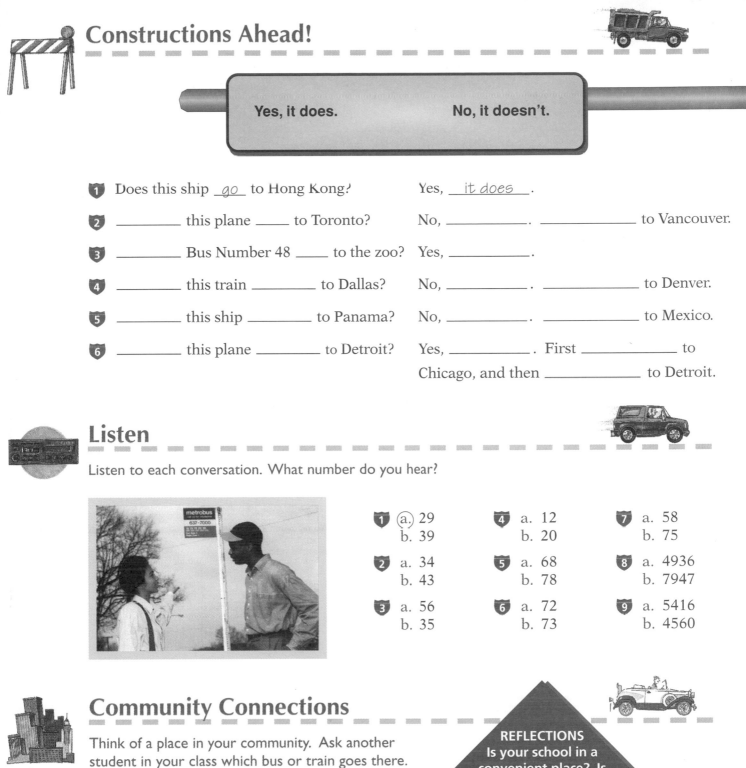

Yes, it does.	No, it doesn't.

1 Does this ship _go_ to Hong Kong? Yes, __it does__.

2 _____ this plane _____ to Toronto? No, _____. _____ to Vancouver.

3 _____ Bus Number 48 _____ to the zoo? Yes, _____.

4 _____ this train _____ to Dallas? No, _____. _____ to Denver.

5 _____ this ship _____ to Panama? No, _____. _____ to Mexico.

6 _____ this plane _____ to Detroit? Yes, _____. First _____ to Chicago, and then _____ to Detroit.

Listen

Listen to each conversation. What number do you hear?

1	a. 29 ⓐ	**4**	a. 12	**7**	a. 58
	b. 39		b. 20		b. 75
2	a. 34	**5**	a. 68	**8**	a. 4936
	b. 43		b. 78		b. 7947
3	a. 56	**6**	a. 72	**9**	a. 5416
	b. 35		b. 73		b. 4560

Community Connections

Think of a place in your community. Ask another student in your class which bus or train goes there. For example:

> *Which bus goes to the library?*

> *Does the D train go to the airport?*

How well do the students in your class know your city or town?

REFLECTIONS
Is your school in a convenient place? Is there public transportation to your school? How do you get there? Is it difficult for some students to get to school? How can your class solve this problem?

Discuss in pairs or small groups, and then share your ideas with the class.

41

A. Is this Bus Number 42?

B. Yes, it is.

A. Oh, good! I'm on the right bus!

A. Does this bus stop at Center Street?

B. Yes, it does.

A. Oh, good! I'm on the right bus!

A. Is this the F train?

B. No, it isn't.

A. Oops! I'm on the wrong train!

A. Does this plane go to Florida?

B. No, it doesn't.

A. Oops! I'm on the wrong plane!

Are you on the right bus, train, or plane? Ask somebody!

Constructions Ahead!

Is this Bus Number 42?	**Yes, it is.**
	No, it isn't.
Does this plane go to Florida?	**Yes, it does.**
	No, it doesn't.

1 Is this the bus to Boston? Yes, __it is__.

2 Does this train go uptown? No, _____. It goes downtown.

3 Is this your telephone number? No, _____.

4 Does this bus stop at the mall? Yes, _____.

5 Is this the train to Tokyo? Yes, _____.

6 Does this plane go to Alabama? No, _____. It goes to Alaska.

Listen

Listen to each question and choose the correct answer.

1
a. Yes, it is.
(b.) Yes, it does.

2
a. No, it doesn't.
b. No, it isn't.

3
a. Yes, it does.
b. Yes, it is.

4
a. No, it isn't.
b. No, it doesn't.

5
a. Yes, it is.
b. Yes, it does.

6
a. No, it doesn't.
b. No, it isn't.

7
a. Yes, it does.
b. Yes, it is.

8
a. No, it isn't.
b. No, it doesn't.

REFLECTIONS
How are the signs on buses or trains in your community? Are they easy to read? Are the signs at bus stops and train stations clear, or are they confusing? Do you sometimes get lost? What do you do when you're lost?

Discuss in pairs or small groups, and then share your ideas with the class.

43

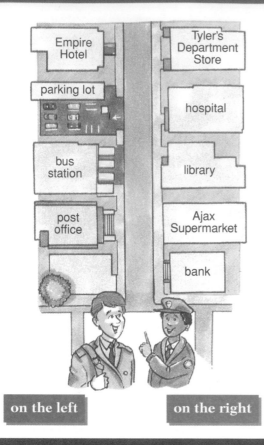

on the left   on the right

the bus station?   the post office

A. Excuse me. Can you tell me how to get to the bus station?

B. Yes. Walk THAT way. The bus station is on the left, next to the post office.

A. I'm sorry. Could you please repeat that?

B. All right. Walk THAT way. The bus station is on the left, next to the post office.

A. Thank you.

1. the library? — the bus station

2. the Empire Hotel? — the parking lot

3. the Ajax Supermarket? — the library and the bank

4. the hospital? — the parking lot

5. Tyler's Department Store? — the hospital

Ask someone you meet on the street for directions.

ExpressWays

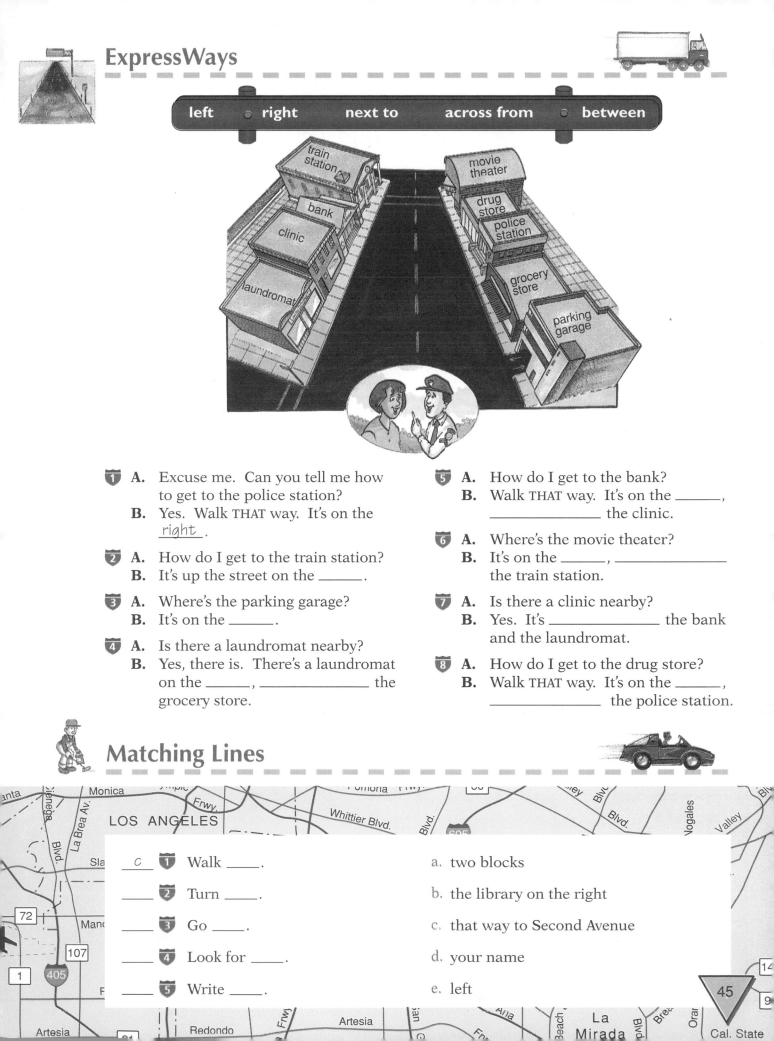

| left | right | next to | across from | between |

1
A. Excuse me. Can you tell me how to get to the police station?
B. Yes. Walk THAT way. It's on the <u>right</u>.

2
A. How do I get to the train station?
B. It's up the street on the _____.

3
A. Where's the parking garage?
B. It's on the _____.

4
A. Is there a laundromat nearby?
B. Yes, there is. There's a laundromat on the _____, _____ the grocery store.

5
A. How do I get to the bank?
B. Walk THAT way. It's on the _____, _____ the clinic.

6
A. Where's the movie theater?
B. It's on the _____, _____ the train station.

7
A. Is there a clinic nearby?
B. Yes. It's _____ the bank and the laundromat.

8
A. How do I get to the drug store?
B. Walk THAT way. It's on the _____, _____ the police station.

Matching Lines

<u>c</u> **1** Walk _____.		a.	two blocks
_____ **2** Turn _____.		b.	the library on the right
_____ **3** Go _____.		c.	that way to Second Avenue
_____ **4** Look for _____.		d.	your name
_____ **5** Write _____.		e.	left

45

A. Excuse me. Can you please tell me how to get to the museum?

B. Yes. Walk that way to Second Avenue and turn right.

A. Uh-húh.

B. Then, go two blocks to Grove Street.

A. Okay.

B. Then, turn left on Grove Street and look for the museum on the right. Have you got that?

A. Yes. Thank you very much.

Ask someone you meet on the street for directions.

ExpressWays

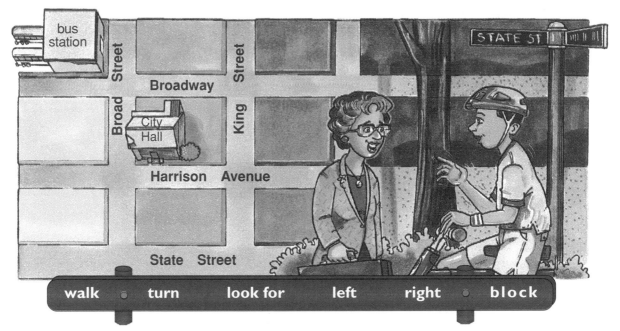

bus station

Broad Street

Broadway

King Street

City Hall

Harrison Avenue

STATE ST

State Street

walk • turn look for left right • block

A. Excuse me. Can you tell me how to get to the bus station?

B. Yes. _____Walk_____¹ that way on State Street. Then _____² right on Broad Street. _____³ two blocks and _____⁴ the bus station on the _____.⁵

A. Excuse me. How do I get to City Hall?

B. _____⁶ that way to Harrison Avenue and turn _____.⁷ Go one _____⁸ and _____⁹ City Hall on the _____.¹⁰

InterActions

Role-play with another student. Draw a map of an area you know—the downtown area of your city or town, or the area near your school.

Another student is "new in town" and asks directions to one of the places on your map. Tell that student how to get there.

Present your role plays to the class. See if other students agree with the directions you give.

REFLECTIONS
Are people on the street helpful when you ask for directions? Do they show you how to get to places? Are they friendly? How are people different in different places you know?

Discuss in pairs or small groups, and then share your ideas with the class.

A. Excuse me. Can you tell me how to get to Franklin's Department Store?

B. Sure. Take the Second Avenue bus and get off at Park Street.

A. I'm sorry. Did you say the Second Avenue bus?

B. Yes. That's right.

A. And WHERE do I get off?

B. At Park Street.

A. Thanks very much.

Listen

Listen to the conversations and choose the correct answer.

1 a. Yes
(b.) No

3 a. Yes
b. No

5 a. Yes
b. No

7 a. Yes
b. No

9 a. Yes
b. No

2 a. Yes
b. No

4 a. Yes
b. No

6 a. Yes
b. No

8 a. Yes
b. No

10 a. Yes
b. No

CrossTalk

You want to go to another student's house, but you need directions:

Can you tell me how to get to your house from here?

The other person gives you directions:

Take . . .   *Get off at . . .*   *Walk . . .*   *Turn right . .*   *Go . . .*

You may need to double-check:

I'm sorry.   *Did you say . . . ?*   *WHERE . . . ?*

With a partner, practice giving directions, and then present your conversations to the class.

Agree or Disagree?

Think of a place in your community and ask someone in the class for directions to get there.

Can you tell me how to get to _____ ?

Take _____ . Get off at _____ .

See if others in the class agree or disagree with the directions.

REFLECTIONS
In your opinion, is it better to walk, drive, or use public transportation to get to places? Why?

Discuss in pairs or small groups, and then share your ideas with the class.

INTERCHANGE

Excuse Me. I'm Lost!

A. Excuse me. I'm lost! Can you possibly tell me how to get to the Holiday Hotel?

B. Sure. Drive that way two miles. Then take the West Side Expressway and get off at Exit 14. Okay so far?

A. Yes. I'm following you.

B. Then turn right at Grand Avenue and look for the Holiday Hotel on the left. Have you got that?

A. Yes. I understand. Thanks very much.

A. Excuse me. I'm lost! Can you possibly tell me how to get to _____?

B. Sure. _____.

Then _____. Okay so far?

A. Yes. I'm following you.

B. Then _____.
Have you got that?

A. Yes. I understand. Thanks very much.

You're going somewhere by car, by public transportation, or on foot . . . and you're lost! Ask someone for directions. Create an original conversation, using the model dialog above as a guide. Feel free to adapt and expand the model any way you wish.

Reading: *Nancy's Neighborhood*

I'm Nancy Warner. I live at 5432 Park Boulevard. I live on the fifth floor of my building. This is my neighborhood. It's really nice! There's a park across from my building. There's a museum next to the park. There's a bus stop across from my apartment. There's a post office nearby, and there's a very nice laundromat between the post office and the drug store. There's also a bank across from the drug store. I like my neighborhood very much. It's very nice, and everything is nearby.

Do You Remember?

Try to answer these questions without looking back at the reading.

1 5432 Park Boulevard is Nancy's _____.
   a. Warner
   (b.) address

2 There's a _____ across from her building.
   a. park
   b. parking lot

3 The museum is _____ the park.
   a. across from
   b. next to

4 There's a _____ across from her apartment.
   a. bus stop
   b. bus station

5 There's a _____ nearby.
   a. movie theater
   b. post office

6 There's a very nice _____ between the post office and the drug store.
   a. laundromat
   b. library

7 There's also a bank _____ the drug store.
   a. around the corner from
   b. across from

8 Nancy likes her neighborhood because _____.
   a. it's on the fifth floor
   b. everything is nearby

Your Turn

For Writing and Discussion

Tell a story about YOUR neighborhood.

Looking Back

☐ **Community**

airport
bank
bus station
clinic
department store
drug store
fire station
gas station
grocery store
hospital
hotel
laundromat

library
movie theater
museum
park
parking lot
police station
post office
shopping mall
supermarket
theater
train station
zoo

☐ **Cardinal Numbers: 20–99**

20 twenty
21 twenty-one
22 twenty-two
23 twenty-three
•   •
•   •
29 twenty-nine
30 thirty
40 forty
50 fifty

60 sixty
70 seventy
80 eighty
90 ninety
99 ninety-nine

☐ **Transportation**

boat
bus
plane
ship
train

expressway
exit

☐ **Ordinal Numbers: 1st–5th**

1st first
2nd second
3rd third
4th fourth
5th fifth

Now Leaving Exit 3 Construction Area

☐ **There Is**
☐ **Prepositions of Location**
☐ **Simple Present Tense**
☐ **Simple Present Tense vs. To Be**
☐ **Short Answers**
☐ **Imperatives**
☐ **WH-Questions**

Sorry for the inconvenience. For more information see page 159.

ExpressWays Checklist

I can . . .

☐ describe the locations of places in the community
☐ access public transportation
☐ give directions to places in the community

REST STOP
Take a break!
Have a conversation!

Here are some scenes from Exits 1, 2, and 3.

Who do you think these people are?
What do you think they're talking about?

In pairs or small groups, create conversations based on these scenes and act them out.

Exit 4

HOUSING AND FOOD

Take Exit 4 to . . .

➔ Identify rooms in the home

➔ Tell about features of an apartment, using *there is/there are* and singular/plural

➔ Discuss rent and utilities

➔ Describe furniture in the home, using *this/that/these/those*

➔ Identify food items, using count/non-count nouns

➔ Locate items in a supermarket, using count/non-count nouns

➔ Discuss ingredients, using count/non-count nouns

Functions This Exit!

Asking for and Reporting Information

Want–Desire

Hesitating

Mr. and Mrs. Park are talking to a realtor about renting an apartment. What do you think they're saying to each other?

Lan is at the supermarket and is asking the stock clerk a question. What do you think they're saying to each other?

A. We're looking for a two-bedroom apartment downtown.

B. I think I have an apartment for you.

A. Oh, good. Can you describe it?

B. Yes. It has two bedrooms, a large living room, and a very nice kitchen.

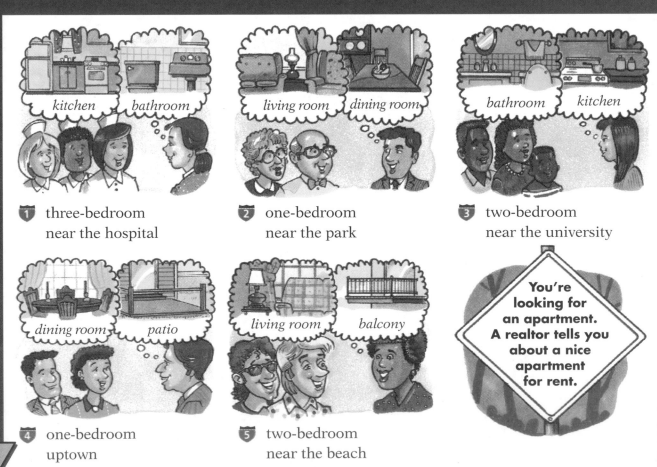

1. three-bedroom
near the hospital

2. one-bedroom
near the park

3. two-bedroom
near the university

4. one-bedroom
uptown

5. two-bedroom
near the beach

You're looking for an apartment. A realtor tells you about a nice apartment for rent.

Let Me Show You Around the Apartment

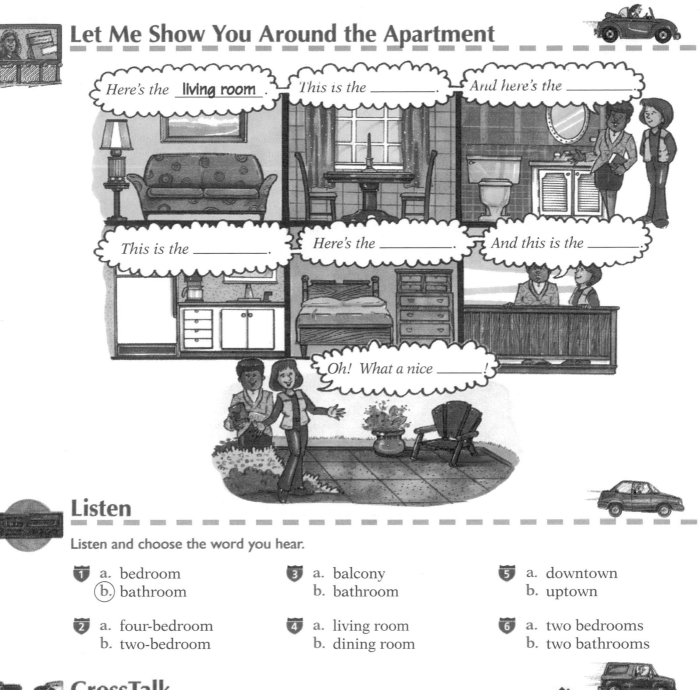

Here's the _living room_.

This is the _____.

And here's the _____.

This is the _____.

Here's the _____.

And this is the _____.

Oh! What a nice _____!

Listen

Listen and choose the word you hear.

1. a. bedroom
   b. bathroom

3. a. balcony
   b. bathroom

5. a. downtown
   b. uptown

2. a. four-bedroom
   b. two-bedroom

4. a. living room
   b. dining room

6. a. two bedrooms
   b. two bathrooms

CrossTalk

Describe your house or apartment to a partner. Have your partner draw a diagram based on your description. For example:

My house has a large living room and two bedrooms.

REFLECTIONS
Are there many apartment buildings in your community? What are good things and bad things about apartment buildings?

Do you live in a house? What are good things and bad things about living in a house?

Discuss in pairs or small groups, and then share your ideas with the class.

A. Is there a refrigerator in the kitchen?

B. Yes, there is. There's a very nice refrigerator in the kitchen.

A. And how many windows are there in the living room?

B. Hmm. Let me see. I think there are four windows in the living room.

Constructions Ahead!

Yes, there is.   Yes, there are.
No, there isn't.   No, there aren't.

1 Is there a closet in the bedroom?   Yes, ____there is____.

2 Are there cabinets in the kitchen?   Yes, _____.

3 Is there a fireplace in the apartment?   No, _____.

4 Are there elevators in the building?   No, _____.

5 Is there a dishwasher in the kitchen?   Yes, _____.

Listen

Someone is calling you about this apartment. Answer the person's questions based on this diagram of the apartment.

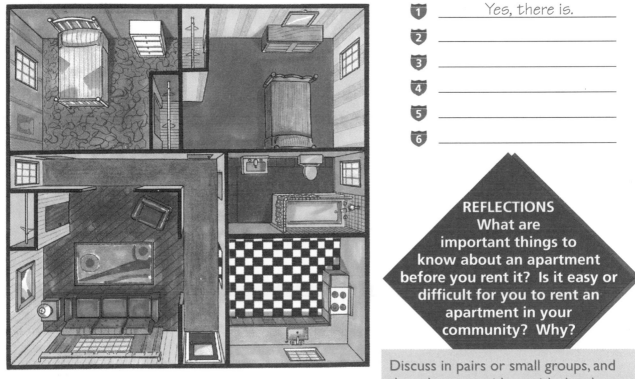

1 ____Yes, there is.____

2 _____

3 _____

4 _____

5 _____

6 _____

REFLECTIONS
What are important things to know about an apartment before you rent it? Is it easy or difficult for you to rent an apartment in your community? Why?

Discuss in pairs or small groups, and then share your ideas with the class.

CrossTalk

Talk with a partner about YOUR house or apartment. Ask each other questions and describe your homes to each other.

Is there a _____?   *Are there _____?*   *How many _____?*

A. How much is the rent?

B. It's $700 a month.

A. Does that include utilities?

B. It includes everything except electricity.

A. Hmm. $700 a month plus electricity?

B. That's right. Do you want to see the apartment?

A. Yes, I think so.

1. $900 / gas

2. $400 / heat

3. $650 / electricity

4. $575 / gas

5. $725 / the parking fee

Ask about the rent and utilities of an apartment you're interested in.

Matching Lines

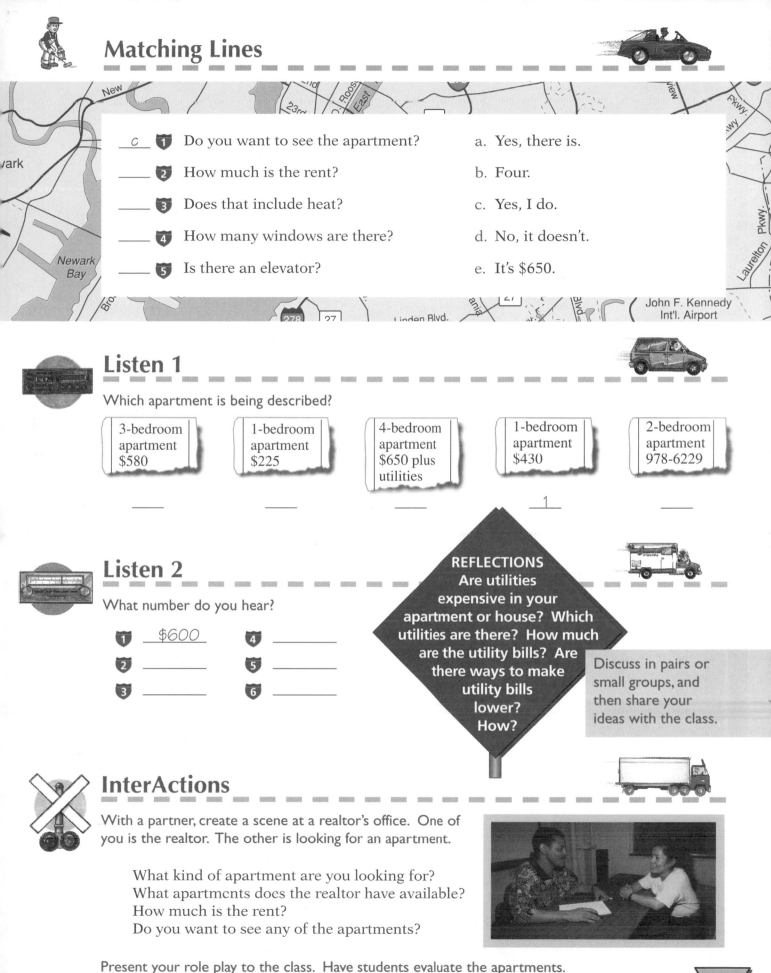

_c_ **1** Do you want to see the apartment?

___ **2** How much is the rent?

___ **3** Does that include heat?

___ **4** How many windows are there?

___ **5** Is there an elevator?

a. Yes, there is.

b. Four.

c. Yes, I do.

d. No, it doesn't.

e. It's $650.

Listen 1

Which apartment is being described?

3-bedroom apartment $580	1-bedroom apartment $225	4-bedroom apartment $650 plus utilities	1-bedroom apartment $430	2-bedroom apartment 978-6229
___	___	___	_1_	___

Listen 2

What number do you hear?

1 _$600_   **4** _____

2 _____   **5** _____

3 _____   **6** _____

REFLECTIONS
Are utilities expensive in your apartment or house? Which utilities are there? How much are the utility bills? Are there ways to make utility bills lower? How?

Discuss in pairs or small groups, and then share your ideas with the class.

InterActions

With a partner, create a scene at a realtor's office. One of you is the realtor. The other is looking for an apartment.

What kind of apartment are you looking for?
What apartments does the realtor have available?
How much is the rent?
Do you want to see any of the apartments?

Present your role play to the class. Have students evaluate the apartments. Is the rent high or low? Are the apartments "worth the money"?

61

A. Where do you want this sofa?

B. That sofa? Hmm. Put it in the living room.

A. And how about these chairs?

B. Those chairs? Let me see. Please put them in the dining room.

Constructions Ahead!

this	these

1. Where do you want __this__ bed?
2. Put _____ lamps in the bedroom.
3. And how about _____ plant?

4. _____ patio is very nice.
5. _____ tables? Put them in the living room.
6. Please put _____ picture near the fireplace.

that	those

7. _____ rug? Put it in the bedroom.
8. _____ pictures are very nice.
9. Where do you want _____ chairs?

10. _____ apartment has three closets.
11. Do you want to see _____ apartment?
12. Put _____ lamps in the living room.

this	that	these	those

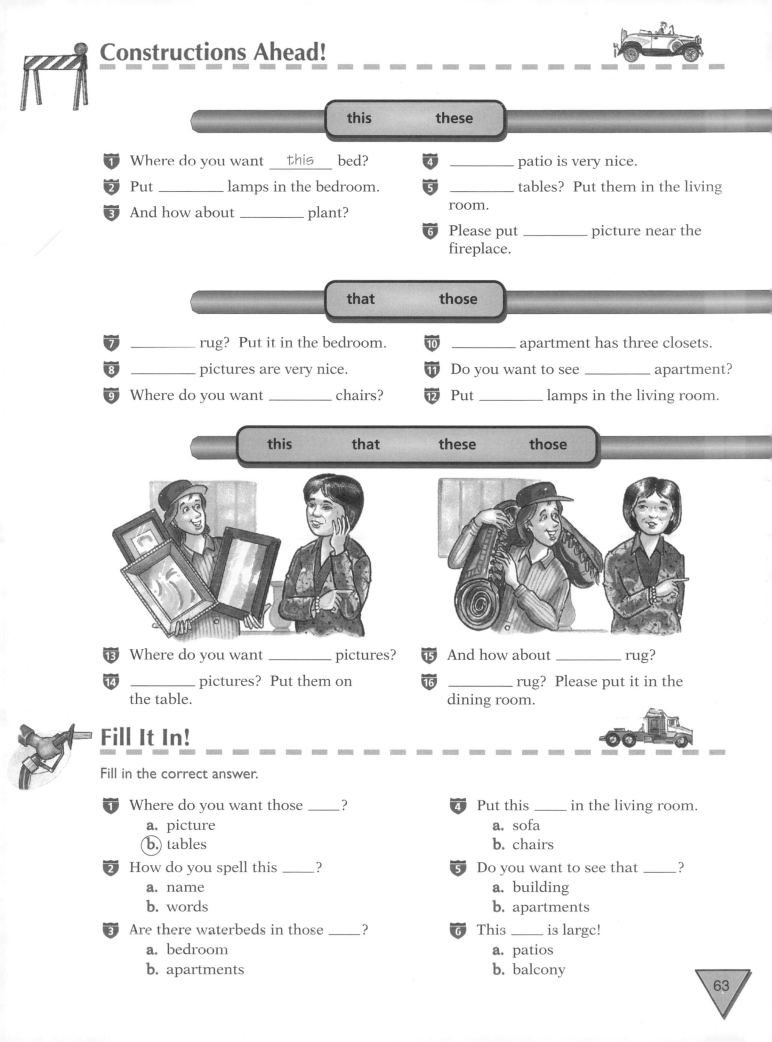

13. Where do you want _____ pictures?
14. _____ pictures? Put them on the table.

15. And how about _____ rug?
16. _____ rug? Please put it in the dining room.

Fill It In!

Fill in the correct answer.

1. Where do you want those _____?
   a. picture
   b.) tables

2. How do you spell this _____?
   a. name
   b. words

3. Are there waterbeds in those _____?
   a. bedroom
   b. apartments

4. Put this _____ in the living room.
   a. sofa
   b. chairs

5. Do you want to see that _____?
   a. building
   b. apartments

6. This _____ is large!
   a. patios
   b. balcony

a cookie

A. What are you looking for?

B. A cookie.

A. I'm afraid there aren't any more cookies.

B. There aren't?

A. No. I'll get some more when I go to the supermarket.

a tomato

1

an apple

2

a banana

3

an egg

4

an orange

5

You're looking in the kitchen for something to eat. There aren't any left!

Listen 1

Listen and choose the correct picture.

1. ☐ ✔ ☐

2. ☐ ☐

3. ☐ ☐

4. ☐ ☐

5. ☐ ☐

6. ☐ ☐

Constructions Ahead!

a cookie	an apple
a tomato	an egg

1. _a_ banana
2. _an_ elevator
3. ____ bus
4. ____ stove
5. ____ apple
6. ____ apartment
7. ____ shower
8. ____ egg
9. ____ rug
10. ____ exit

Listen 2

Which word do you hear?

1. a. tomato
   (b.) tomatoes

2. a. refrigerator
   b. refrigerators

3. a. egg
   b. eggs

4. a. cookie
   b. cookies

5. a. banana
   b. bananas

6. a. neighborhood
   b. neighborhoods

7. a. orange
   b. oranges

8. a. chair
   b. chairs

9. a. elevator
   b. elevators

A. What are you looking for?

B. Milk.

A. I'm afraid there isn't any more milk.

B. There isn't?

A. No. I'll get some more when I go to the supermarket.

1. bread

2. cheese

3. lettuce

4. ice cream

5. coffee

You're looking in the kitchen for something to eat. There isn't any left!

isn't   aren't

1. I'm afraid there _isn't_ any more milk in the refrigerator.

2. There _____ any eggs. Sorry!

3. There _____ any more coffee.

4. There _____ any lettuce for a sandwich.

5. I'm afraid there _____ any nice tomatoes.

6. There _____ any more cookies in the kitchen.

7. I'm sorry. There _____ any more bread.

8. There _____ any cheese in the house.

9. There _____ any more oranges. Sorry!

Figure It Out!

Look in your refrigerator and make a list of all the foods you have there. Your partner will try to guess 10 things that are in your refrigerator. For example:

Is there any cheese in your refrigerator?

Are there any eggs in your refrigerator?

REFLECTIONS
Which snack foods are good for you? Which snack foods are bad for you? Why?

Discuss in pairs or small groups, and then share your ideas with the class.

See how many foods each of you can guess correctly!

A. Excuse me. Where are the carrots?

B. They're in Aisle J.

A. I'm sorry. Did you say "A"?

B. No. "J."

A. Oh. Thank you.

A. Excuse me. Where's the butter?

B. It's in Aisle 3.

A. I'm sorry. Did you say "C"?

B. No. "3."

A. Oh. Thanks.

You're looking for something in a supermarket. Ask the clerk where it is.

Crossed Lines

Put the following lines in the correct order.

____ No. "2."

__1__ Excuse me. I'm looking for tofu.

____ I'm sorry. Did you say "D"?

____ It's in Aisle "2."

____ They're in Aisle "3."

____ And where are the bean sprouts?

____ No. "3."

____ I'm sorry. Did you say "Q"?

Listen

What numbers and letters do you hear?

1 ⑧ H	**4** E G	**7** A J
2 B D	**5** 3 C	**8** 16 10C
3 N M	**6** 9 19	**9** 18 8D

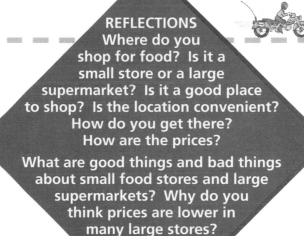

REFLECTIONS
Where do you shop for food? Is it a small store or a large supermarket? Is it a good place to shop? Is the location convenient? How do you get there? How are the prices?

What are good things and bad things about small food stores and large supermarkets? Why do you think prices are lower in many large stores?

Discuss in pairs or small groups, and then share your ideas with the class.

Community Connections

Visit a local supermarket or grocery store. Make a list of five products you find in each of the following sections of the store. Compare your list with other students' lists.

Baking Supplies	Bread and Baked Goods	Coffee and Tea	Dairy Products

Fish and Seafood	Fruit and Vegetables	Frozen Foods	Meat and Poultry

69

Mmm! This Cake Is Delicious!

A. Mmm! This cake is delicious!

B. I'm glad you like it.

A. What's in it?

B. Let me think . . . some eggs, some sugar, some flour, and some raisins.

A. Well, it's excellent!

B. Thank you for saying so.

A. Mmm! These egg rolls are delicious!

B. I'm glad you like them.

A. What's in them?

B. Let me see . . . some cabbage, some pork, some shrimp, and some bean sprouts.

A. Well, they're excellent!

B. Thank you for saying so.

You're eating at a friend's home. The food is delicious. Compliment your friend, using the model dialogs above as a guide. Feel free to adapt and expand the models any way you wish.

Matching Lines

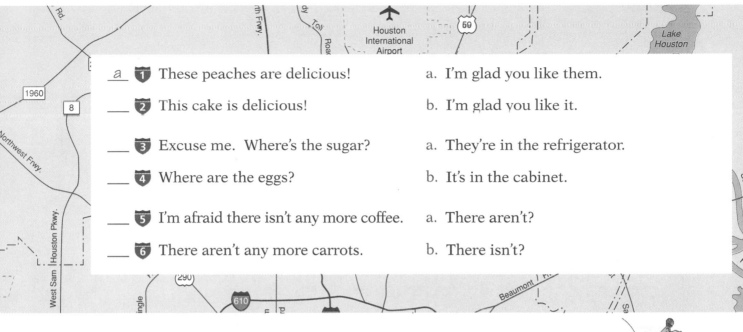

a **1** These peaches are delicious!

2 This cake is delicious!

a. I'm glad you like them.

b. I'm glad you like it.

3 Excuse me. Where's the sugar?

4 Where are the eggs?

a. They're in the refrigerator.

b. It's in the cabinet.

5 I'm afraid there isn't any more coffee.

6 There aren't any more carrots.

a. There aren't?

b. There isn't?

Reading: *Jim's New Apartment*

This is Jim's new one-bedroom apartment. It's downtown in a very convenient location. He's showing his new apartment to his friend Tom. The apartment has a living room with a large window. There's a very nice kitchen with a dishwasher, a large refrigerator, and lots of cabinets. There's a shower in the bathroom, and the bedroom has a nice large closet. The rent is $450 dollars a month, and that includes utilities.

Tom is looking for a new apartment. Fortunately, there are two vacant apartments in the building. Maybe Jim will have a new neighbor!

Yes, No, or Maybe?

1 Jim likes his new apartment.

2 It's in the center of the city.

3 Jim's living room is large.

4 There's a window in the kitchen.

5 The apartment has a dishwasher.

6 There's a lot of room to put food in Jim's kitchen.

7 The apartment has two bedrooms.

8 There's a closet in Jim's bedroom.

9 Jim's apartment also has a nice balcony.

10 Tom wants to move to a new apartment.

11 There are two apartments for rent in the building.

12 Tom might move into Jim's building.

Looking Back

Housing
balcony
bathroom
bedroom
dining room
kitchen
living room
patio

cabinet
closet
dishwasher
fireplace
refrigerator
shower

stove
window

apartment
building
elevator
floor
parking lot
parking space

electricity
gas
heat
parking fee
rent
utilities

☐ **Furniture**
bed
chair
crib
lamp
picture
plant
rug
sofa
table
TV
waterbed

☐ **Foods**
apple
banana
bean sprouts
bread
butter
cabbage
cake
carrot
cheese
coffee
cookie
egg
egg rolls

flour
ice cream
lettuce
milk
orange
peach
pork
potato
raisins
rice
shrimp
sugar
tomato
yogurt

☐ **Community**
beach
hospital
park
supermarket
university

Now Leaving Exit 4 Construction Area

☐ **Singular/Plural**
☐ **Count/Non-Count Nouns**
☐ **This/That/These/Those**
☐ **Articles: A/An, The**
☐ **Some/Any**
☐ **Imperatives**
☐ **Have/Has**
☐ **Simple Present Tense vs. To Be**

Sorry for the inconvenience. For more information see page 160.

ExpressWays Checklist

I can . . .

☐ identify rooms in the home
☐ tell about the features of an apartment
☐ discuss rent and utilities
☐ describe furniture in the home
☐ identify food items
☐ locate items in a supermarket
☐ discuss ingredients

Exit 5

AT WORK

Take Exit 5 to . . .

↗ Describe occupations, using the simple present tense

↗ Tell about work skills, using *can* and *can't*

↗ Describe people, using adjectives

↗ Ask for and give feedback at work, using the present continuous tense and object pronouns

↗ Tell about everyday activities, using the simple present tense and days of the week

↗ Tell about family dynamics, using adverbs of frequency

↗ Discuss recreation, using *like*

Functions This Exit!

Asking for and Reporting
   Information
Ability/Inability
Describing
Approval/Disapproval
Requests
Gratitude

Roberta and Abraham are friends. They're talking about their jobs and the jobs of people in their families. What do you think they're saying to each other?

A person at an employment agency is asking Ricardo about his job skills. What do you think they're saying to each other?

teach

A. What do you do?

B. I'm a teacher.

A. Oh, really? What do you teach?

B. I teach Biology.

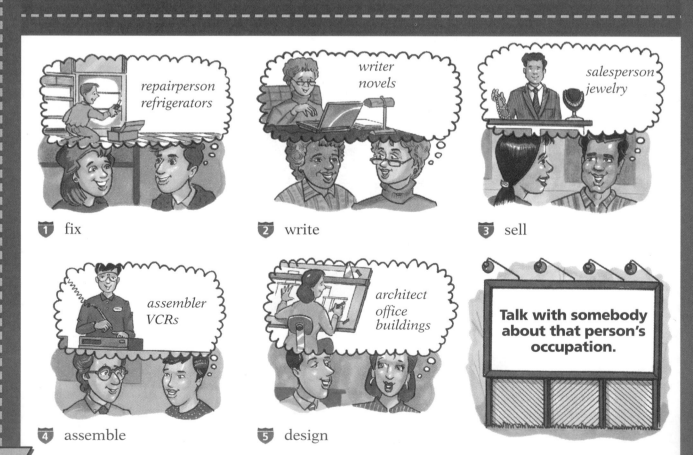

1 fix

2 write

3 sell

4 assemble

5 design

Talk with somebody about that person's occupation.

74

Constructions Ahead!

What do { I / we / you / they } do?   { I / We / You / They } work.

write • fix   sell   design   assemble • teach

1. I'm a salesperson. ___I___ ___sell___ children's clothing.
2. My wife and I are teachers. _____ _____ English literature at the high school.
3. I'm a writer. _____ _____ short stories.
4. I'm a repairperson. _____ _____ television sets at Fred's Fix-It Shop.
5. We're architects. _____ _____ bridges.
6. Marta and Kim are assemblers. _____ _____ toys at the We "R" Toys factory.

What's the Question?

1. What ___do you sell___ ?   I sell cars and trucks.
2. Where _____ ?   I work at the State Street Bank.
3. What_____ ?   We fix cars and trucks.
4. What _____ ?   I teach Japanese.
5. What _____ ?   They design office buildings.
6. Where _____ ?   We work at the Midtown Mall.

75

your husband
Where does he work?

A. What does your husband do?

B. He's a chef.

A. That's interesting. Where does he work?

B. He works at the Lakeview Restaurant.

your wife
What languages does she speak?

A. What does your wife do?

B. She's a bilingual secretary.

A. That's interesting. What languages does she speak?

B. She speaks English and Spanish.

1 your brother
Where does he work?

2 your sister
Where does she work?

3 your father
What does he deliver?

4 your mother
Where does she work?

5 your son
What instrument does he play?

Ask about people's occupations.

Constructions Ahead!

What does { he / she } do?   { He / She } works/sells/fixes.

write   sell   assemble   work   design
speak   play   deliver   fix

1. Alice is a musician. _She_ _plays_ the piano.

2. My daughter is a bilingual secretary. _____ _____ English and Japanese.

3. My son is an architect. _____ _____ factories and office buildings.

4. Mike is an assembler. _____ _____ radios.

5. Carol is a delivery person. _____ _____ furniture.

6. Harry is a security guard. _____ _____ at the Pandex Corporation.

7. My husband is a writer. _____ _____ novels.

8. Jack is a mechanic. _____ _____ cars and trucks at Al's Auto Repair.

9. Irene is a salesperson. _____ _____ jewelry and watches.

Listen

Listen and choose the correct answer.

1. a. fix cars
   b. fixes cars

2. a. sell jewelry
   b. sells jewelry

3. a. teach Biology
   b. teaches Biology

4. a. assemble VCRs
   b. assembles VCRs

5. a. speak English and Chinese
   b. speaks English and Chinese

6. a. write novels
   b. writes novels

7. a. deliver furniture
   b. delivers furniture

8. a. design office buildings
   b. designs office buildings

Your Turn

For Writing and Discussion

Tell about the occupations of people in your family.

What do the people in your family do?
Where do they work?
What do they do at work?

REFLECTIONS
In your opinion,
what are some good
occupations? Why?
What are some bad
occupations? Why?

Discuss in pairs or small groups, and
then share your ideas with the class.

77

fix cars

speak French

A. Can you fix cars?

B. Yes, I can. I'm an experienced mechanic.

A. Can you speak French?

B. No, I can't. But I'm sure I can learn quickly.

1 assemble toys

2 fix television sets

3 design bridges

4 teach History

5 play the piano

Ask about somebody's skills.

78

Constructions Ahead!

| I He She It We You They | can/can't work. |

Can you work?
Yes I can.
No, I can't.

1 Can you play the piano? — No, _I can't_. But _I can play_ the guitar.

2 Can Mr. Taylor teach Biology? — No, _____. But _____ Chemistry.

3 Can these architects design bridges? — No, _____. But _____ factories.

4 Can Maria speak Greek? — No, _____. But _____ Spanish.

5 Can you and Jack fix refrigerators? — No, _____. But _____ cars.

6 Can you assemble television sets? — No, _____. But _____ VCRs.

Your Turn

For Writing and Discussion

I can sing.   *I can't dance.*   *I can use a computer.*   *I can't fix a car.*

How about you? What can you do? What can't you do? Make a list and then compare your list with other students' lists. See who can do what!

Five Things I Can Do!	Five Things I Can't Do!
. . . .	. . . .
. . . .	. . . .
. . . .	. . . .
. . . .	. . . .
. . . .	. . . .

REFLECTIONS
In your opinion, what are the most important skills people need today to get good jobs? How do people get these skills?

Discuss in pairs or small groups, and then share your ideas with the class.

A. Please give this to Mr. Hernandez in the Personnel Office.

B. I'm sorry, but I'm new here. What does he look like?

A. He's short, with black hair.

B. Okay. I'll do it right away.

Mr. Hernandez in the Personnel Office

He's short, with black hair.

height	weight	hair	
very tall	very thin	curly	brown
tall	thin	straight	black
average height	heavy		blond/blonde
short	very heavy	dark	red
very short		light	gray

Ms. Kramer on the first floor

1 She's tall, with blonde hair.

Mrs. Cummings in Shipping

2 She's average height, with gray hair.

Henry in the mailroom

3 He's heavy, with curly dark hair.

Mr. Malone in the cafeteria

4 He's very tall and thin.

Miss Newman on the third floor

5 She's short, with straight brown hair.

You're supposed to give something to a person at work, but you don't know what the person looks like.

80

ExpressWays

1 Is Ms. Green tall?   No. She's _____short_____.

2 Is Michael heavy?   No. He's _____.

3 Is your hair curly   No. It's _____.

4 Is Carol's hair dark?   No. It's _____.

5 Is Mr. Maxwell very tall?   No. He's very _____.

6 Is Irene short?   No. She's _____.

7 Is her hair straight?   No. It's _____.

8 Is your son's hair light?   No. It's _____.

Crossed Lines

Put the following lines in the correct order.

____ In the Shipping Department.

____ Is his hair curly?

____ I'm sorry, but I'm new here. Where does he work?

____ On the first floor.

_1_ Please give this package to Mr. Morrison.

____ He's tall, with light brown hair.

____ Tell me, what does Mr. Morrison look like?

____ Where's the Shipping Department?

____ No. It's straight.

Your Turn

For Writing and Discussion

Write a description of yourself.

    Are you tall or short? Are you heavy or thin? Is your hair curly or straight? Is it black, brown, blond, red, or gray?

Give your description to another student and have that student read it to the class. See if people can guess "who's who" based on the descriptions.

REFLECTIONS
The first days in a new job are sometimes difficult. There are new people to meet, new places to locate, and new things to learn. Tell about your first days on a job.

Discuss in pairs or small groups, and then share your ideas with the class.

give this presentation
it

A. Am I giving this presentation all right?

B. Yes, you are. You're giving it very well.

A. Thanks.

1 stock the shelves
them

2 shampoo Mrs. Baxter
her

3 guard the president
him

4 defend you
me

5 train you
us

Ask for feedback. Ask
somebody how you're doing.

Constructions Ahead!

I	me
he	him
she	her
it	it
we	us
you	you
they	them

1 Do you fix cars?

Yes. I fix _them_ every day.

2 Am I assembling this refrigerator all right?

You're assembling _____ very well.

3 Does your boss compliment you very often?

Yes. She compliments _____ all the time.

4 Are you training Michael, the new mechanic?

Yes. I'm training _____ this week.

5 Can you help Ms. Peterson deliver the mail?

Yes. I can help _____ right now.

6 Does your supervisor meet with you and your co-workers very often?

Yes. He meets with _____ every week.

7 I'm on vacation this week. Do you miss me?

Yes. We miss _____ very much.

Community Connections

Visit a workplace in your community. Observe and take notes.

What kinds of jobs are there?
What are people doing?
In your opinion, how are they doing their jobs?

Report to the class and discuss with other students the many kinds of jobs and work activities at these workplaces.

REFLECTIONS
The people on page 82 are asking for feedback. Why is it important to do this? Do you ask for feedback at school, at work, or at home? What do you ask about?

Discuss in pairs or small groups, and then share your ideas with the class.

What Day Is It?

go to computer class

Monday

A. Are you busy after work today?

B. Hmm. What day is it?

A. It's Monday.

B. I'm afraid I'm busy. I go to a computer class on Monday.

take guitar lessons

1 Tuesday

work out at the gym

2 Wednesday

visit my grandmother at the nursing home

3 Thursday

volunteer at the hospital

4 Friday

coach my daughter's soccer team

5 Saturday

You're busy today.
What day is it?

Your Turn

For Writing and Discussion

Tell something you do on each day of the week.

On Monday I ....

On Tuesday I ....

On Wednesday I ....

On Thursday I ....

On Friday I ....

On Saturday I ....

On Sunday I ....

Compare your list with other students' lists.

CrossTalk

What's your favorite day of the week?

My favorite day of the week is Monday. On Monday morning I play tennis in the park with my friends.

My favorite day of the week is Wednesday. Every Wednesday afternoon I volunteer at the local hospital.

My favorite day of the week is Friday. Every Friday evening I have dinner with my son and his wife.

My favorite day of the week is Saturday. On Saturday night I go to the movies with my friends.

How about you? What's your favorite day of the week? Talk with a partner and then report to the class about your favorite day.

85

100%	**always**
↕	**usually**
	often
	sometimes
	rarely
0%	**never**

A. How often do you talk to your kids in college?

B. We usually call them on Sunday evenings.

A. Do they ever call you?

B. Never. We always call them.

A. Do you and your girlfriend see each other often?

B. Not really. We always go out on Saturday nights, but we rarely see each other the rest of the week.

A. Why?

B. She usually does her homework after school, and I'm always at football practice. We never see each other on weekday evenings because we both work.

A. How often do you see your parents?

B. Not very often. They live far away.

A. Do you and your family go to visit them?

B. Sometimes, but we usually talk to them on the telephone.

A. Do they ever visit you?

B. No. They rarely visit us. We usually visit them.

What friends and family members do you keep in touch with? Do you call? Do you write? Do you visit? How often? Talk with a partner about people you keep in touch with.

Reading: *My Best Friend*

Eileen Rogers is my best friend. We're both from Chicago, but now I live in San Francisco and Eileen lives in Atlanta. We don't see each other very often, but we're in touch all the time. I often write to Eileen and tell her about all the things that are happening at the Ajax Company. I'm the office manager there. And she often writes to me about her work at the Valley Hospital. She's a doctor there.

We talk on the telephone once a week, either on Saturday or Sunday morning. There are also other ways we communicate with each other. Sometimes I call her on her car phone, or she faxes me on my fax machine. And when I have something very important to tell her, I sometimes beep her on her beeper.

We're really lucky. In this new age of communication, there are so many ways we can keep in touch with each other. We live in different cities on different coasts, but we're in touch all the time.

How Often?

1. These two friends _____ see each other.
   - a. usually
   - (b.) rarely

2. They _____ write to each other.
   - a. often
   - b. never

3. They _____ talk to each other on the weekend.
   - a. never
   - b. always

4. They _____ use a fax machine or a beeper to communicate with each other.
   - a. sometimes
   - b. usually

5. They _____ lose touch with each other.
   - a. often
   - b. never

6. These friends are lucky because _____ .
   - a. they live in different cities
   - b. there are many ways to keep in touch

Your Turn

For Writing and Discussion

Complete the following any way you wish and then compare with a partner.

I always . . . .

I usually . . . .

I often . . . .

I sometimes . . . .

I rarely . . . .

I never . . . .

INTERCHANGE

What Kind of TV Shows Do You Like?

A. What kind of TV shows do you like?

B. I like news programs. How about you?

A. I like game shows.

B. What's your favorite program?

A. "Guess the Price!" How about you?

B. "Newsmakers."

A. What kind of _____ do you like?

B. I like _____. How about you?

A. I like _____.

B. What's/Who's your favorite _____?*

A. _____. How about you?

B. _____.

REFLECTIONS
Why do you think making small talk is important at work or at school? What subjects do people talk about? What subjects are not good for small talk? What questions are too personal? Are there differences between small talk in different cultures? Describe any differences you know.

You're taking a break at work, and you and a co-worker are "making small talk" about TV shows, movies, music, and sports. Create original conversations, using the vocabulary and questions on page 89 and the model dialog above as a guide. Feel free to adapt and expand the model any way you wish.

Discuss in pairs or small groups, and then share your ideas with the class.

TV Shows

situation comedies/
sitcoms

dramas

talk shows

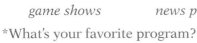

game shows

news programs

children's programs

*What's your favorite program?

Movies

dramas

comedies

westerns

cartoons

adventure movies

science fiction movies

*Who's your favorite movie star?

Music

classical music

popular music

rock music

country music

jazz

rap music

*Who's your favorite performer?

Sports

baseball

basketball

football

hockey

soccer

*What's your favorite team?

89

Looking Back

☐ **Job Skills**
assemble
deliver
design
fix
guard
play
sell
speak
stock
teach
work
write

☐ **Occupations**
architect
assembler
baker
chef
delivery person
mechanic
musician
repairperson
salesperson
secretary
security guard
teacher
writer

☐ **Days of the Week**
Monday
Tuesday
Wednesday
Thursday
Friday
Saturday
Sunday

☐ **Sports**
baseball
basketball
football
hockey
soccer

☐ **Describing People**
height
very tall
tall
average height
short
very short
weight
very thin
thin
heavy
very heavy

hair
curly
straight
dark
light
brown
black
blond/blonde
red
gray

Now Leaving Exit 5 Construction Area

☐ **Simple Present Tense**
☐ **Can**
☐ **Adjectives**
☐ **Object Pronouns**
☐ **Adverbs of Frequency**

Sorry for the inconvenience. For more information see page 161.

ExpressWays Checklist
I can . . .
☐ describe occupations
☐ talk about work skills
☐ describe people
☐ ask for and give feedback at work
☐ tell about everyday activities
☐ tell about family dynamics
☐ discuss recreation

90

Exit 6

HEALTH AND EMERGENCIES

Take Exit 6 to . . .

➔ Identify common ailments, using *have*

➔ Ask for recommendations and locate items in a drug store

➔ Make a doctor's appointment, using time expressions

➔ Give a medical history, using *to be* and the simple present tense

➔ Follow instructions during a medical exam, using imperatives

➔ Receive a doctor's medical advice with *should*

➔ Receive a pharmacist's directions for taking medication

➔ Report an emergency

Functions This Exit!

Asking for and Reporting
   Information
Instructing
Advice–Suggestions
Directions–Location
Checking and Indicating
   Understanding
Initiating a Topic

Beverly doesn't feel very well. She's talking to the receptionist at the doctor's office and is making an appointment. What do you think they're saying to each other?

Dr. Lee is giving some medical advice to his patient. What do you think they're saying to each other?

a headache

A. You know … you don't look very well.
Are you feeling okay?

B. No, not really.

A. What's the matter?

B. I have a headache.

A. I'm sorry to hear that.

an earache

1

a stomachache

2

a toothache

3

a sore throat

4

a backache

5

A friend isn't feeling very well. Ask what's wrong.

Constructions Ahead!

$$\begin{Bmatrix} I \\ We \\ You \\ They \end{Bmatrix} \text{ have} \quad \begin{Bmatrix} He \\ She \\ It \end{Bmatrix} \text{ has}$$

1 My brother _____has_____ an earache.

2 I _____ a toothache.

3 You _____ a sore throat.

4 Carol and Jessica _____ stomachaches.

5 Anna and I _____ headaches.

6 Rick _____ a backache.

What's the Matter?

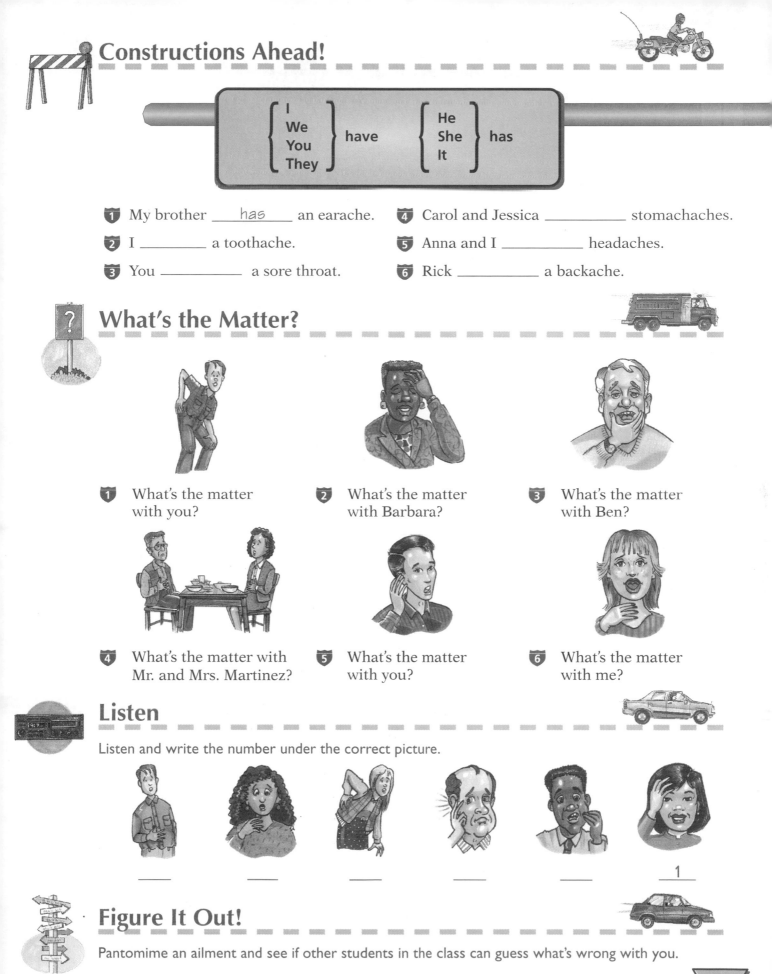

1 What's the matter with you?

2 What's the matter with Barbara?

3 What's the matter with Ben?

4 What's the matter with Mr. and Mrs. Martinez?

5 What's the matter with you?

6 What's the matter with me?

Listen

Listen and write the number under the correct picture.

____ ____ ____ ____ ____ _1_

Figure It Out!

Pantomime an ailment and see if other students in the class can guess what's wrong with you.

a bad cold | Maxi-Fed Cold Medicine

in Aisle 2 on the right

A. Excuse me. Can you help me?

B. Yes.

A. I have a bad cold. What do you recommend?

B. I recommend Maxi-Fed Cold Medicine.

A. Maxi-Fed Cold Medicine?

B. Yes.

A. Where can I find it?

B. It's in Aisle 2 on the right.

A. Thanks.

a backache | Brown's Pain Pills

in Aisle 3 on the top shelf

A. Excuse me. Can you help me?

B. Yes.

A. I have a backache. What do you recommend?

B. I recommend Brown's Pain Pills.

A. Brown's Pain Pills?

B. Yes.

A. Where can I find them?

B. They're in Aisle 3 on the top shelf.

A. Thank you.

a headache | Taylor's Aspirin

1 in Aisle 1 on the left

a stomachache | Tummy-Aid Tablets

2 in Aisle 4 on the bottom shelf

an earache | Drum's Ear Drops

3 in Aisle 2 on the middle shelf

a bad cough | Silence Cough Syrup

4 in the back near the aspirin

a terrible sore throat | Victor's Throat Lozenges

5 in the front near the cash register

You're at the drug store. Ask a pharmacist to recommend some medicine.

Fill It In!

Fill in the correct answer.

My Medicine Cabinet

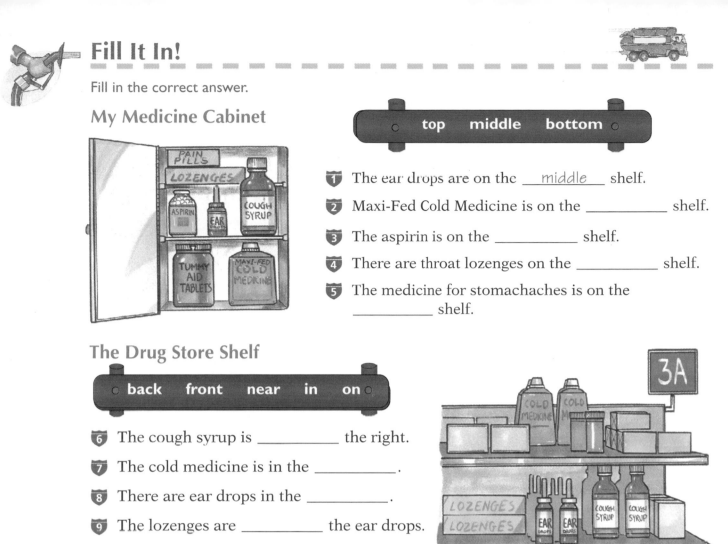

| top | middle | bottom |

1. The ear drops are on the ___middle___ shelf.
2. Maxi-Fed Cold Medicine is on the _____ shelf.
3. The aspirin is on the _____ shelf.
4. There are throat lozenges on the _____ shelf.
5. The medicine for stomachaches is on the _____ shelf.

The Drug Store Shelf

| back | front | near | in | on |

6. The cough syrup is _____ the right.
7. The cold medicine is in the _____.
8. There are ear drops in the _____.
9. The lozenges are _____ the ear drops.
10. These items are _____ Aisle 3A.

Community Connections

Visit a local drug store and ask the pharmacist what he or she recommends for the following ailments: a cold, a headache, a stomachache, a cough, an earache, a toothache, and a backache. Report your findings to the class and compare recommendations.

Cultural Intersections

Different cultures have "home remedies" for common ailments. For example:

For a stomachache, I recommend very strong tea.

For a headache, I recommend a hot shower.

Talk with a partner about YOUR recommendations for common ailments — either favorite medications or "home remedies" you know of.

A. Doctor's office.

B. Hello. This is John Stevens. I'm not feeling very well.

A. What's the problem?

B. My right foot hurts very badly.

A. I see. Do you want to make an appointment?

B. Yes, please.

A. Can you come in tomorrow morning at 9:00?*

B. Tomorrow morning at 9:00? Yes. That's fine. Thank you.

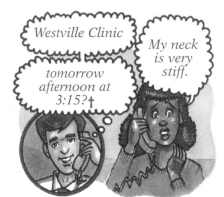

1 Karen Fuller isn't feeling very well.

2 Sally Wilson's son isn't feeling very well.

3 Mr. Beck's daughter isn't feeling very well.

4 Ms. Wong isn't feeling very well.

5 Charlie Green's parrot, Willy, isn't feeling very well.

MAKE AN APPOINTMENT TO SEE THE DOCTOR.

* 9:00 = nine o'clock
† 3:15 = three fifteen
** 4:30 = four thirty
†† 11:45 = eleven forty-five

What Time Is It?

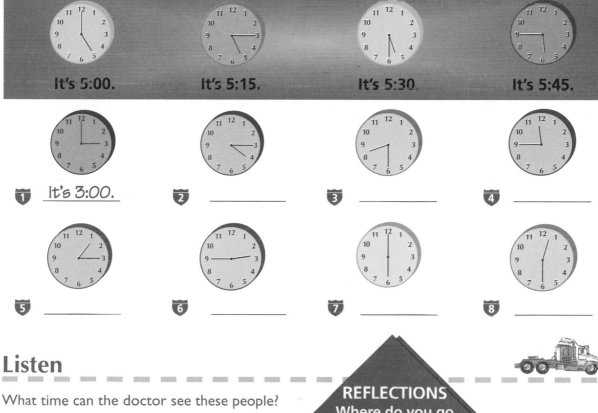

It's 5:00. It's 5:15. It's 5:30 It's 5:45.

1 It's 3:00. **2** _____ **3** _____ **4** _____

5 _____ **6** _____ **7** _____ **8** _____

Listen

What time can the doctor see these people?

1 10:15 **5** _____

2 _____ **6** _____

3 _____ **7** _____

4 _____ **8** _____

Crossed Lines

Oh, no! There's a problem with the telephone.
Put the following lines in the correct order.

____ What's the matter?

____ This afternoon at 3:45? Okay. Thank you.

____ Hello. This is Mrs. King. I'm not feeling
very well.

____ I have a terrible backache.

____ Yes, please.

_1_ Bayside Medical.

____ Can you come in this afternoon at 3:45?

____ I see. Do you want to make
an appointment to see a doctor?

REFLECTIONS
Where do you go
for medical care? Do
you make an appointment
or do you just walk in? Are you
satisfied with the medical care you
and your family members
receive? Are there any
problems? What can
you do about
them?

REFLECTIONS
Many people don't
go for medical care when
they have a minor problem.
They wait, and then they go to a
hospital emergency room when the
problem is serious.   Why do you
think people do this? Why
do you think this is a
problem?

Discuss in pairs or small groups, and
then share your ideas with the class.

97

A. I have just one more question.

B. All right.

A. Do you smoke?

B. No, I don't.

A. Okay. I think that's all the information I need for your medical history. The doctor will see you shortly.

B. Thank you.

ExpressWays

| I do | I am | there is | there are |
| I don't | I'm not | there isn't | there aren't |

1 Are you feeling well?   No, _I'm not_ .

2 Are you having problems with your ears?   Yes, _____ .

3 Do you exercise regularly?   No, _____ .

4 Is there a history of heart disease in your family?   No, _____ .

5 Do you have any allergies?   Yes, _____ .

6 Are you taking any medication?   No, _____ .

7 Are there any more questions?   No, _____ .

Listen

Listen to the conversation and answer these questions.

1   a. The patient smokes.
    (b.) The patient doesn't smoke.

2   a. She's allergic to aspirin.
    b. She's allergic to penicillin.

3   a. She drinks alcohol.
    b. She doesn't drink alcohol.

4   a. She exercises regularly.
    b. She doesn't exercise regularly.

5   a. There's a history of heart disease in her family.
    b. There isn't a history of heart disease in her family.

6   a. She has a stomachache.
    b. She has a sore throat.

7   a. She's taking medication.
    b. She isn't taking any medication.

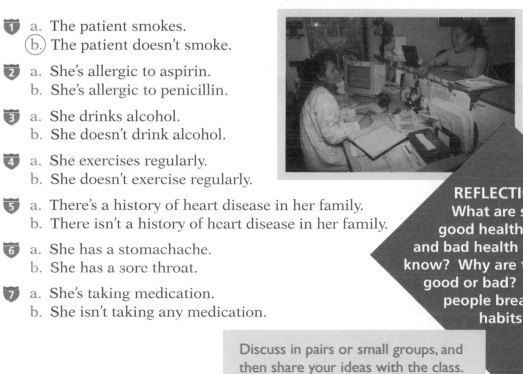

REFLECTIONS
What are some good health habits and bad health habits you know? Why are these habits good or bad? How can people break bad habits?

Discuss in pairs or small groups, and then share your ideas with the class.

99

*Touch **your** toes.*

A. Touch your toes.

B. My toes?

A. Yes.

*Take off **your** shirt.*

A. Take off your shirt.

B. My shirt?

A. Yes.

*Sit **on the** table.*

A. Sit on the table.

B. On the table?

A. Yes.

*Hold **your** breath.*

A. Hold your breath.

B. Hold my breath?

A. Yes.

*Lie **on your back**.*

1

*Look **at the ceiling**.*

2

Cough.

3

*Roll up **your sleeve**.*

Say "a-a-h"!

4

5

The doctor is giving you a physical examination.

_c_ **1** Touch ____.

____ **2** Roll up ____.

____ **3** Hold ____.

____ **4** Lie ____.

____ **5** Look at ____.

a. the ceiling

b. on your back

c. your toes

d. your sleeve

e. your breath

Do What the Doctor Says!

Give others directions for doing things. When you begin with "The doctor says ...," the person must do what you say. For example:

> *The doctor says "Touch your toes."*

> *The doctor says "Look at the ceiling."*

When you don't say "The doctor says ...," the person should NOT do what you say. Whoever follows your instructions when you don't say "The doctor says ..." is out of the game.

REFLECTIONS
How often should people have a regular physical examination? Why is this important? When was your last physical exam?

Discuss in pairs or small groups, and then share your ideas with the class.

Here are some other words and expressions you might like to use in the game:

right arm

left arm

right leg

left leg

elbow

knee

eye

nose

Stand up.

Sit down.

Turn around.

Raise ____.

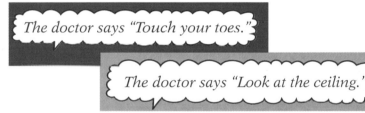

weight
go on a diet
lose 15 pounds

A. I'm concerned about your weight.

B. My weight?

A. Yes. You should go on a diet.

B. I see.

A. I suggest that you lose 15 pounds.

B. I understand. Thank you for the advice.

1 lungs
stop smoking
quit immediately

2 back
exercise daily
do sit-ups

3 blood pressure
change your diet
stop eating salty and
fatty foods

4 gums
use dental floss
use it daily

5 life style
slow down
take a vacation

Your doctor is giving you
some medical advice.

Good Advice

Choose the best advice for these medical conditions.

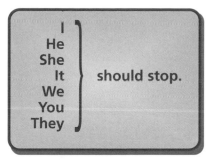

| I |
| He |
| She |
| It | should stop. |
| We |
| You |
| They |

1 I suggest that you lose 15 pounds. You should _____.
   a. slow down
   (b.) go on a diet

2 I'm concerned about Mr. Chen's blood pressure. He should _____.
   a. change his diet
   b. use dental floss

3 The doctor is concerned about our lungs. He says we should _____.
   a. quit smoking
   b. take a vacation

4 I'm concerned about their gums. They should _____.
   a. do sit-ups
   b. use dental floss

5 I'm concerned about her back. She should _____.
   a. stop eating
   b. exercise daily

6 My doctor is concerned about my blood pressure. She says I should _____.
   a. eat fatty foods
   b. stop eating salty foods

CrossTalk

With a partner, discuss which of the following are good or bad for a person's health. Report to the class about your discussion and compare ideas.

Exercise daily.

Eat meat daily.

Smoke.

Sleep 8 hours every night.

Eat fruit and vegetables every day.

Take a shower every morning.

Take a vacation once a year.

Drink a lot of coffee and tea.

Your Turn

For Writing and Discussion

In your opinion, what should a person do to stay healthy?

A. Here's your medicine.

B. Thank you.

A. Be sure to follow the directions on the label. Take one tablet three times a day.

B. I understand. One tablet three times a day.

A. That's right.

Match the Labels

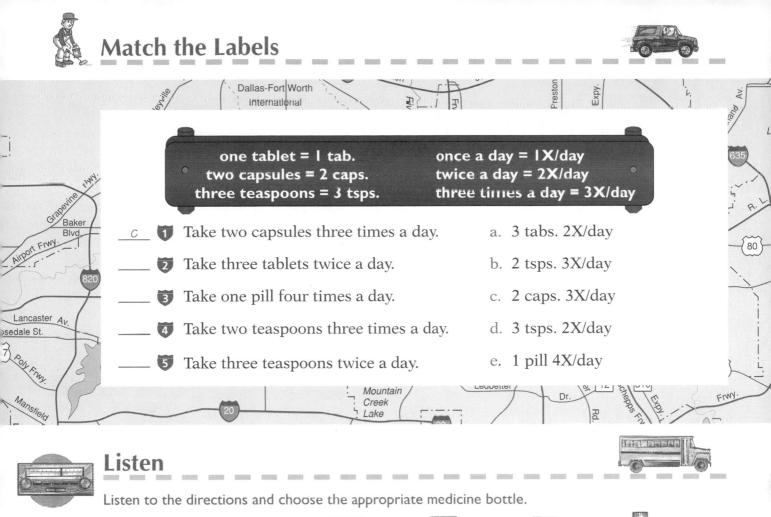

one tablet = 1 tab.	once a day = 1X/day
two capsules = 2 caps.	twice a day = 2X/day
three teaspoons = 3 tsps.	three times a day = 3X/day

_c_  **1** Take two capsules three times a day.

____ **2** Take three tablets twice a day.

____ **3** Take one pill four times a day.

____ **4** Take two teaspoons three times a day.

____ **5** Take three teaspoons twice a day.

a. 3 tabs. 2X/day

b. 2 tsps. 3X/day

c. 2 caps. 3X/day

d. 3 tsps. 2X/day

e. 1 pill 4X/day

Listen

Listen to the directions and choose the appropriate medicine bottle.

1 cap. 3X/day	2 caps. 2X/day	3 tabs. 2X/day	1 pill 4X/day	1 pill 1X/day	1 tsp. 2X/day
____	____	____	_1_	____	____

Your Turn

For Writing and Discussion

Complete the following and discuss with a partner. Compare your ideas and then report to the class.

When I have a stomachache, I . . . .

When I have a toothache, I . . . .

When I have a sore throat, I . . . .

When I have a backache, I . . . .

When I have an earache, I . . . .

When I have an allergic reaction to something, I . . . .

When my doctor gives me advice, I . . . .

When the pharmacist gives me advice, I . . . .

INTERCHANGE

I Want to Report an Emergency!

A. Police.

B. I want to report an emergency!

A. Yes?

B. I think my father is having a heart attack!

A. What's your name?

B. Diane Perkins.

A. And the address?

B. 76 Lake Street.

A. Telephone number?

B. 293-7637.

A. All right. We'll be there right away.

B. Thank you.

Diane Perkins
76 Lake Street
293-7637

1 Neal Stockman
193 Davis Avenue
458-9313

2 Carla Martinez
17 Park Road
963-2475

3 Carol Weaver
440 Lexington Boulevard
354-6260

4 Henry Stewart
5 Linden Lane
723-0980

You're reporting an emergency. Create an original conversation, using the model dialog above as a guide. Feel free to adapt and expand the model any way you wish.

Reading: *Call 911*

Carol Davis is an operator, but she doesn't work at the telephone company. She works at the Police Emergency Unit in her city. People call "9-1-1" and speak to her when they want to report an emergency. Carol is very busy right now. A man thinks there is a burglar in his apartment. He's telling Carol his name, address, and telephone number.

Diane Stewart also works at the Police Emergency Unit. She's busy, too. A woman is reporting a medical emergency. The woman's husband is having a heart attack. Diane is calling the hospital. An ambulance will be there right away.

Now somebody is reporting a new emergency to Carol. An apartment building downtown is on fire! Carol is calling the fire department. They'll be there right away.

Carol and Diane like their jobs. They like to help people, and their work is very exciting.

What's the Answer?

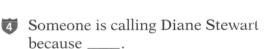

1 Carol Davis _____ at the telephone company.
   a. works
   b.) doesn't work

2 The Police Emergency Unit number is _____.
   a. 9-1-1
   b. an emergency

3 Someone is calling Carol because _____.
   a. he's a burglar
   b. he hears a burglar

4 Someone is calling Diane Stewart because _____.
   a. she's having a heart attack
   b. her husband is having a heart attack

5 Diane is _____.
   a. sending an ambulance
   b. calling "9-1-1"

6 Carol is now sending the fire department downtown because _____.
   a. Diane is calling the fire department
   b. an apartment building is on fire

InterActions

With a small group of students, pantomime an emergency situation. See if the rest of the class can guess what the situation is.

Looking Back

Health
allergies
backache
bleeding
choking
cold
cough
dizzy
earache
headache
heart attack
heart disease
sore throat

stiff neck
stomachache
toothache

back
ear
foot
gums
lungs
neck
toes

blood pressure
diet
life style
weight

Medicine
aspirin
cold medicine
cough syrup
ear drops
medication
penicillin
throat lozenges
capsule
pill
tablet
teaspoon

Personal Information
name
address
telephone number

Emergencies
ambulance
emergency
fire department
hospital
police
police emergency
  unit

Family Members
daughter
father
son
wife

Now Leaving Exit 6 Construction Area

☐ **Imperatives**
☐ **Have/Has**
☐ **Time Expressions**
☐ **Should**
☐ **Simple Present Tense vs. To Be**
☐ **Count/Non-Count Nouns**
☐ **Short Answers**
☐ **Possessive Nouns**

Sorry for the inconvenience. For more information see page 162.

ExpressWays Checklist
I can . . .
☐ identify common ailments
☐ ask for recommendations and locate items in a drug store
☐ make a doctor's appointment
☐ give a medical history
☐ follow instructions during a medical exam
☐ receive a doctor's medical advice
☐ receive a pharmacist's directions for taking medication
☐ report an emergency

Here are some scenes from Exits 4, 5, and 6.

Who do you think these people are?
What do you think they're talking about?

In pairs or small groups, create conversations based on these scenes and act them out.

Exit 7

SHOPPING

Take Exit 7 to . . .

- ↗ Ask for articles of clothing in a department store, using singular/plural
- ↗ Select articles of clothing by size and color
- ↗ Find the right article of clothing, using singular/plural and adjectives
- ↗ Locate items and facilities in a department store, using ordinal numbers
- ↗ Purchase items in a department store
- ↗ Return items to a department store, using adjectives
- ↗ Use the services of a post office

Functions This Exit!

Want–Desire
Directions–Location
Satisfaction/Dissatisfaction
Attracting Attention
Gratitude
Checking and Indicating
  Understanding
Hesitating

A salesperson is helping this customer in a department store. What do you think they're saying to each other?

Diane is talking to a clerk at the post office. What do you think they're saying to each other?

a shirt — *in Aisle 3*

A. Excuse me. Can you help me?
B. Certainly.
A. I'm looking for a shirt.
B. Shirts are in Aisle 3.
A. Thank you.

a tie — *on that counter*

A. Excuse me. Can you help me?
B. Certainly.
A. I'm looking for a tie.
B. Ties are on that counter.
A. Thank you.

a dress — *over there*

A. Excuse me. Can you help me?
B. Certainly.
A. I'm looking for a dress.
B. Dresses are over there.
A. Thank you.

a pair of pants — *on that rack*

A. Excuse me. Can you help me?
B. Certainly.
A. I'm looking for a pair of pants.
B. Pants are on that rack.
A. Thank you.

1. *a coat* — *on that rack*
2. *an umbrella* — *on that counter*
3. *a blouse* — *over there on that table*
4. *a pair of shoes* — *in the front of the store*
5. *a hat* — *in the back of the store*

You're looking for one of the items of clothing at the top of the next page.

More Clothing

sweater

jacket

suit

vest

jersey

bathrobe

raincoat

sweatshirt

evening gown

(pair of) pajamas

sneakers

boots

rubbers

ExpressWays

1. This ((dress) dresses) is very nice.
2. Where are the (coat coats)?
3. I'm looking for a (bathrobe bathrobes).
4. (Umbrella Umbrellas) are on that table.
5. I recommend this (tie ties) with that shirt.
6. What a nice pair of (suits boots)!
7. Are you looking for a (vest vests)?
8. (Pajamas Bathrobe) are over there.
9. This pair of (sneakers blouse) is very nice.
10. Excuse me. Where are (shirt sweatshirts)?

REFLECTIONS
What are some good places to buy clothing in your community? Why are these good places to shop?

Discuss in pairs or small groups, and then share your ideas with the class.

Figure It Out!

Take turns pantomiming someone either putting on or holding an article of clothing. See if other students in your class can guess what the article of clothing is.

113

red   pink   orange   yellow   green   blue   purple

black   white   gray

brown   gold   silver

*a belt
size 36
black*

A. May I help you?

B. Yes, please. I'm looking for a belt.

A. What size do you want?

B. Size 36.

A. And what color?

B. Black.

A. Okay. Let's see . . . a size 36 black belt.
Here you are.

B. Thank you very much.

*a sweater
medium
green*

*a raincoat
small
brown*

*pants
size 34
gray*

1   **2**   **3**

*a long-sleeved
shirt
size 15½*
yellow*

*socks
extra-large
red, white,
and blue*

**You're looking for
something in a
department store.**

4   **5**

* 15½ = fifteen and a half

What Are They Wearing?

Brian is wearing _____

_____

_____

_____

_____

_____

_____

Julie is wearing _____

_____

_____

_____

_____

_____

_____

_____

How about you? What are YOU wearing today?

....

....

....

....

....

Listen

What article of clothing do you hear?

1 a. sweater
   b. sweaters

2 a. tie
   b. ties

3 a. shirt
   b. shirts

4 a. dress
   b. dresses

5 a. blouse
   b. blouses

6 a. belt
   b. belts

7 a. coat
   b. coats

8 a. raincoat
   b. raincoats

9 a. pair of socks
   b. pairs of socks

Figure It Out!

Describe what a student in your class is wearing and see if others can guess who it is. For example:

She's wearing a blue and white blouse and a red skirt.

He's wearing a yellow shirt and brown pants.

jacket

A. How does the jacket fit?

B. It's too short.

A. Do you want to try on another one?

B. Yes, please.

A. Okay. Here. I think this jacket will fit better.

B. Thanks very much.

pants

A. How do the pants fit?

B. They're too long.

A. Do you want to try on another pair?

B. Yes, please.

A. Okay. Here. I think these pants will fit better.

B. Thanks very much.

1 skirt

2 sneakers

3 blouse

4 gloves

5 suit

You're trying something on in a department store, and it doesn't fit.

ExpressWays

This • These is • are

1. <u>This</u> raincoat _____ too long!

2. _____ sneakers _____ too big!

3. _____ blouse _____ too large!

4. _____ gloves _____ too tight!

5. _____ jacket _____ too tight!

6. _____ suit _____ too short!

What's the Sound?

Say these words and put them in the correct column.

pants   raincoats   blouses   socks   ties
shoes   offices   dresses   sweaters

s	z	IZ
pants	shoes	offices

Listen

Listen and choose the appropriate picture.

1. ✔ _____   _____

2. _____   _____

3. _____   _____

4. _____   _____

5. _____   _____

6. _____   _____

on the 4th floor

the rest rooms?

in the back of the store

the elevator?

A. Excuse me. Where are the rest rooms?

B. They're on the fourth floor.

A. The fourth floor?

B. Yes.

A. Thanks.

A. Excuse me. Where's the elevator?

B. It's in the back of the store.

A. The back of the store?

B. Yes.

A. Thanks.

on the 1st floor

refrigerators?

1

near the elevator

the dressing room?

2

on the 3rd floor

TVs and radios?

3

on the 2nd floor

bedroom furniture?

4

in the basement

the Customer Service Counter?

5

You need directions in a department store.

118

The Department Store Directory

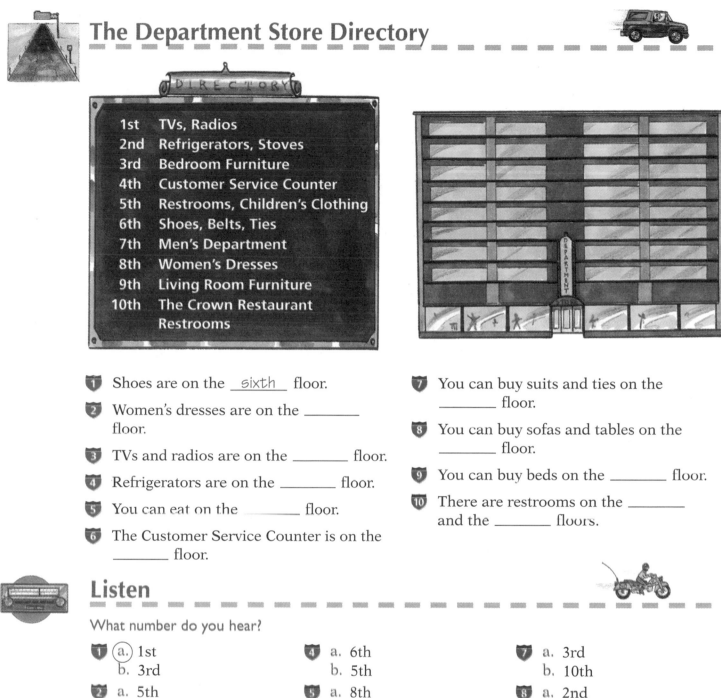

DIRECTORY

1st	TVs, Radios
2nd	Refrigerators, Stoves
3rd	Bedroom Furniture
4th	Customer Service Counter
5th	Restrooms, Children's Clothing
6th	Shoes, Belts, Ties
7th	Men's Department
8th	Women's Dresses
9th	Living Room Furniture
10th	The Crown Restaurant Restrooms

1. Shoes are on the __sixth__ floor.

2. Women's dresses are on the _____ floor.

3. TVs and radios are on the _____ floor.

4. Refrigerators are on the _____ floor.

5. You can eat on the _____ floor.

6. The Customer Service Counter is on the _____ floor.

7. You can buy suits and ties on the _____ floor.

8. You can buy sofas and tables on the _____ floor.

9. You can buy beds on the _____ floor.

10. There are restrooms on the _____ and the _____ floors.

Listen

What number do you hear?

1. a. 1st (circled)
   b. 3rd

2. a. 5th
   b. 9th

3. a. 7th
   b. 10th

4. a. 6th
   b. 5th

5. a. 8th
   b. 10th

6. a. 4th
   b. 5th

7. a. 3rd
   b. 10th

8. a. 2nd
   b. 7th

9. a. 1st
   b. 5th

Community Connections

Make a list of nine items or locations a person might look for in a department store. For example:

bedroom furniture	TVs	refrigerators
rugs	restrooms	shirts
sneakers	restaurant	Customer Service

Exchange your list with another student. Then visit a local department store and find out where each of these can be found in the store. Report your findings to the class.

119

A. I'd like to buy this watch.

B. Okay. That's twenty-six ninety-five ($26.95).

A. Excuse me, but I don't think that's the right price. I think this watch is on sale this week.

B. Oh. You're right. It's ten percent (10%) off. I'm sorry.

A. That's okay.

B. With the tax, that comes to twenty-five dollars and forty-six cents ($25.46).

A. I'd like to buy these earrings.

B. Okay. That's twelve fifty ($12.50).

A. Excuse me, but I don't think that's the right price. I think these earrings are on sale this week.

B. Oh. You're right. They're half price. I apologize.

A. That's okay.

B. With the tax, that comes to six dollars and fifty-six cents.

1 necklace

2 boots

3 camera

4 stockings

5 typewriter

YOU'RE BUYING SOMETHING IN A DEPARTMENT STORE.

What's That Number?

> *That's fifteen thirty-four.*

1 (a.) $15.34
  b. $153.34

> *That's twenty seven sixty.*

2 a. $20.76
  b. $27.60

> *That comes to sixty-nine fifty-eight.*

3 a. $69.58
  b. $695.08

> *That comes to five hundred twenty-six dollars and eleven cents.*

4 a. $526.11
  b. $500.27

> *With the tax, that comes to two hundred thirty dollars and twenty cents.*

5 a. $203.20
  b. $230.20

> *That's forty-three ninety-nine, and that includes tax.*

6 a. $43.99
  b. $403.99

Listen

What amount do you hear?

1 ___$11.15___   **3** _____   **5** _____

2 _____   **4** _____   **6** _____

Community Connections

Visit a local department store. Look for ten items you would like to buy. Describe each item and write down its price.

Report back to the class and have students decide whether or not the items are worth the money.

REFLECTIONS
Do you look for sales at stores before you go shopping? How do you find out about sales? Do you buy things right away, or do you wait for things to go on sale? How much money can you save when you buy things on sale?

Discuss in pairs or small groups, and then share your ideas with the class.

ExpressWays

1. These boots are half price. Now they're ___$25.00___ .

2. Typewriters are 10% off. Now they're _____ .

3. Cameras are 50% off. That comes to _____ .

4. Jackets are on sale. They're 10% off. Now that comes to _____ .

5. These sweaters are half price. That's _____ .

6. Blouses are 10% off this week. That comes to _____ .

Community Connections

Look in a newspaper and cut out an advertisement for a product that is on sale.

On the board, make a list of all the students' products. Write down what the prices were, what they are now, and what the discount is. For example:

Product	Previous Price	New Price	Discount
Sony CD player	$160	$120	25% off

Decide with the class which product is the "best buy" this week!

InterActions

Create an advertisement for a product, using the following as a guide, and then present your ad to the class.

Come to _____!

This week we're having a sale on _____ .

All our _____s are _____ .

_____ is on _____ Street in _____ .

We're open from _____ to _____, _____ through _____ .

So come to _____ and buy a _____ at only _____!

Reading: *Shopping in Department Stores*

Department stores in the United States are very large. They're called department stores because they have many different departments. For example, you can buy dresses, blouses, and skirts in the Women's Clothing Department. You can buy suits, shirts, and ties in the Men's Clothing Department. Parents can buy clothing for their children in the Children's Clothing Department. And shoes, boots, and sneakers are in the Shoe Department.

Most department stores have TVs and radios in their Home Entertainment Departments. Some stores also have Appliance Departments. You can buy refrigerators, stoves, dishwashers, and other appliances there.

Do you want to read a book? Go to the Book Department! Do you want to buy a pair of earrings or a necklace? Go to the Jewelry Department! Do you want to buy some special chocolate? Go to the Gourmet Food Department!

There are a lot of other reasons why people shop in department stores. You can buy things at special low prices when department stores have sales. Sometimes stores even have half-price sales!

You can also return things at department stores. Take your receipt to the Customer Service Department, and you can exchange the item or get a refund. In some stores, you can even eat lunch or dinner in a restaurant.

Department stores are great places to shop because people can get almost everything they want in one place.

True or False?

1. You can buy dresses in the Women's Clothing department.
2. You can buy skirts and ties in the Men's Clothing department.
3. Most department stores sell television sets.
4. Some department stores sell home appliances.
5. If you want to buy a watch, go to the Gourmet Food department.
6. You can save money when the store has a sale.
7. If you want to return something, go to the Customer Service department.

CrossTalk

Talk with a partner about your favorite department store. Where is it? What do you usually buy there?

fan
noisy

A. I want to return this fan.

B. What's the matter with it?

A. It's too noisy.

B. Do you want to exchange it?

A. No. I'd like a refund, please.

B. Okay. Do you have the receipt?

A. Yes. Here you are.

jeans
short

A. I want to return these jeans.

B. What's the matter with them?

A. They're too short.

B. Do you want to exchange them?

A. No. I'd like a refund, please.

B. Okay. Do you have the receipt?

A. Yes. Here you are.

1 purse
small

2 pajamas
tight

3 coat
heavy

4 videogames
easy

5 textbook
difficult

You want to return something in a department store.

ExpressWays

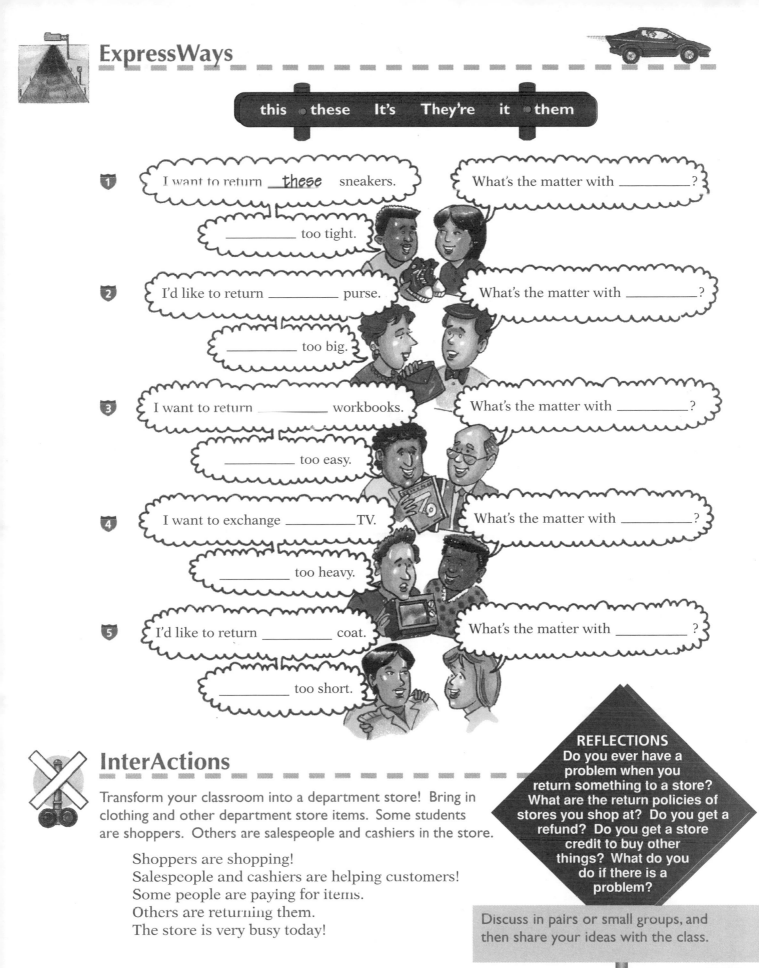

| this • these | It's | They're | it • them |

1 I want to return __these__ sneakers.

What's the matter with _____?

_____ too tight.

2 I'd like to return _____ purse.

What's the matter with _____?

_____ too big.

3 I want to return _____ workbooks.

What's the matter with _____?

_____ too easy.

4 I want to exchange _____ TV.

What's the matter with _____?

_____ too heavy.

5 I'd like to return _____ coat.

What's the matter with _____?

_____ too short.

InterActions

Transform your classroom into a department store! Bring in clothing and other department store items. Some students are shoppers. Others are salespeople and cashiers in the store.

Shoppers are shopping!
Salespeople and cashiers are helping customers!
Some people are paying for items.
Others are returning them.
The store is very busy today!

REFLECTIONS
Do you ever have a problem when you return something to a store? What are the return policies of stores you shop at? Do you get a refund? Do you get a store credit to buy other things? What do you do if there is a problem?

Discuss in pairs or small groups, and then share your ideas with the class.

buy some stamps

A. I want to buy some stamps, please.

B. I'm sorry. You're at the wrong window.
You can buy stamps at Window Number 2.

A. Window Number 2?

B. Yes.

A. Thank you.

1 mail a package

2 buy a money order

3 send a registered letter

4 buy an aerogramme

5 file a change of address form

You're at the post office.

Fill It In!

Fill in the correct answer.

1. I'd like to mail a _____.
   a. stamp
   b. registered letter ✓

2. I'd like to buy some _____, please.
   a. stamps
   b. change of address forms

3. I'd like a _____, please.
   a. registered letter
   b. money order

4. I'd like to _____ this letter to Hong Kong.
   a. file
   b. mail

5. Can I file a _____ at this window?
   a. package
   b. change of address form

6. I'd like to send a _____.
   a. package
   b. stamp

7. I want to buy this _____.
   a. package
   b. aerogramme

8. You can buy stamps at the next _____.
   a. post office
   b. window

Listen

Listen and choose the appropriate picture.

_____   _____   _____

_____   1   _____

Cultural Intersections

Every country has many beautiful and interesting stamps. Bring to class some stamps you have saved. Tell what country they're from. Describe and compare them with stamps other students bring to class.

Which stamp is the most beautiful? the most interesting? the most unusual?

Who are the people on the stamps?

INTERCHANGE

I'd Like to Mail This Package

A. I'd like to mail this package.

B. Where's it going?

A. To Detroit.

B. How do you want to send it?

A. First class, please.

B. Do you want to insure it?

A. Hmm. I don't know.

B. Well, is it valuable?

A. Yes, it is. It's a camera I'm sending to my brother. Please insure it for fifty dollars ($50).

B. All right. That's four dollars and thirty-seven cents ($4.37), please.

A. I'd like to mail this package.

B. Where's it going?

A. To _____.

B. How do you want to send it?

A. First class, please.

B. Do you want to insure it?

A. Hmm. I don't know.

B. Well, is it valuable?

A. Yes, it is. It's a _____ I'm sending to _____.
Please insure it for _____ dollars.

B. All right. That's _____ dollars and _____ cents, please.

You're mailing a package at the post office. Create an original conversation, using the model dialog above as a guide. Feel free to adapt and expand the model any way you wish.

128

Matching Lines

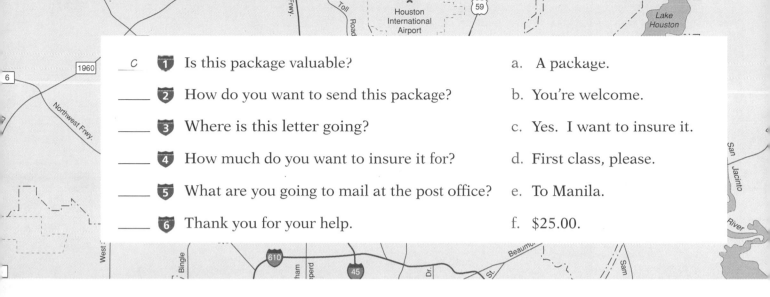

_c_ **1** Is this package valuable?

a. A package.

____ **2** How do you want to send this package?

b. You're welcome.

____ **3** Where is this letter going?

c. Yes. I want to insure it.

____ **4** How much do you want to insure it for?

d. First class, please.

____ **5** What are you going to mail at the post office?

e. To Manila.

____ **6** Thank you for your help.

f. $25.00.

Listen

Listen and choose the correct response.

1 a. First class, please.
    (b.) To Toronto.

5 a. Thanks very much.
    b. Certainly.

2 a. First class.
    b. Today.

6 a. Over there.
    b. That's $4.00.

3 a. Yes, it is.
    b. No, there aren't.

7 a. No, they aren't.
    b. I'd like a refund.

4 a. No, I don't.
    b. Yes, I am.

8 a. All right.
    b. I don't know.

Community Connections

Think of some questions for another student in your class to ask at the post office. For example:

How many postal workers are at your local post office?

How much does it cost to send a letter to _____ ?
                                              (you decide where)

How much does it cost to send a _____ pound/kilogram package
  to _____ ?
    (you decide where)

How much does it cost to send an overnight letter to _____ ?

Exchange questions with another student. Everybody should go to a post office and ask their questions. As a class, compare information about the post offices and postal services.

129

Looking Back

For more information see page 163.

☐ **Clothing**
bathrobe
belt
blouse
coat
dress
evening
  gown
hat
jacket
necklace
purse
raincoat
rubbers

shirt
skirt
suit
sweater
sweatshirt
tie
umbrella
vest
watch
boots
earrings
gloves
jeans
pajamas

pants
shoes
sneakers
socks
stockings

☐ **Department Store**
aisle
basement
counter
Customer
  Service
  Counter

dressing
  room
elevator
price
rack
receipt
refund
restrooms
sale
table
tax

☐ **Colors**
black
blue
brown
gold
gray
green
orange
pink
purple
red
silver
white
yellow

☐ **Describing**
big
difficult
easy
heavy
large
long
noisy
short
small
tight

☐ **Post Office**
aerogramme
change of
  address
  form
money order
package
registered
  letter
stamps
first class
insure
window

Now Leaving Exit 7 Construction Area

☐ **Singular/Plural**
☐ **Adjectives**
☐ **Too + Adjective**
☐ **Prepositions of Location**
☐ **WH-Questions**

Sorry for the inconvenience. For more information see page 163.

ExpressWays Checklist

I can . . .

☐ ask for articles of clothing in a department store
☐ select articles of clothing by size and color
☐ find the right article of clothing
☐ locate items and facilities in a department store
☐ purchase items in a department store
☐ return items to a department store
☐ use the services of a post office

Exit 8

RECREATION

Take Exit 8 to . . .

➔ Tell about weekend plans, using *going to*

➔ Make plans for the day, using *want to* and weather expressions

➔ Make and respond to invitations, using *can't* and *have to*

➔ Tell about weekend activities, using the past tense

➔ Make plans for the day, using *want to*

➔ Share information, using *to be* in the past

➔ Tell about things you *like to* do

Functions This Exit!

Want–Desire
Asking for and Reporting
    Information
Intention
Invitations
Obligations
Likes/Dislikes

Dorothy and Carmen are talking during a break at work about their weekends. What do you think they're saying to each other?

Amir is inviting Nicole to do something, but she can't because she's busy. What do you think they're saying to each other?

see a play

go dancing

A. What are you going to do this weekend?

B. I'm going to go dancing. How about you?

A. I'm going to see a play.

B. Well, have a good weekend!

A. You, too.

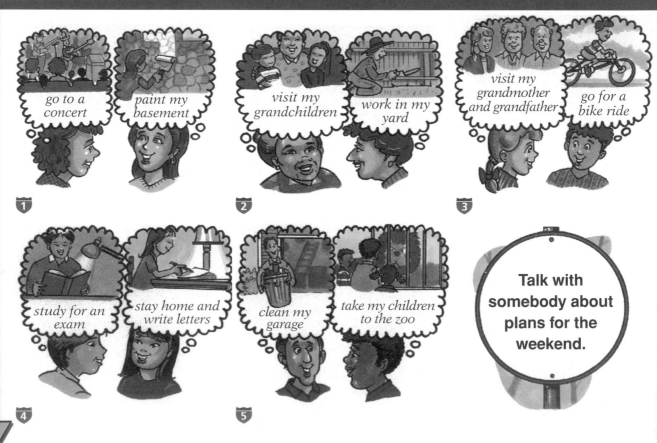

1. go to a concert / paint my basement

2. visit my grandchildren / work in my yard

3. visit my grandmother and grandfather / go for a bike ride

4. study for an exam / stay home and write letters

5. clean my garage / take my children to the zoo

Talk with somebody about plans for the weekend.

Constructions Ahead!

I'm
He's
She's
We're
You're
They're
} going to study.

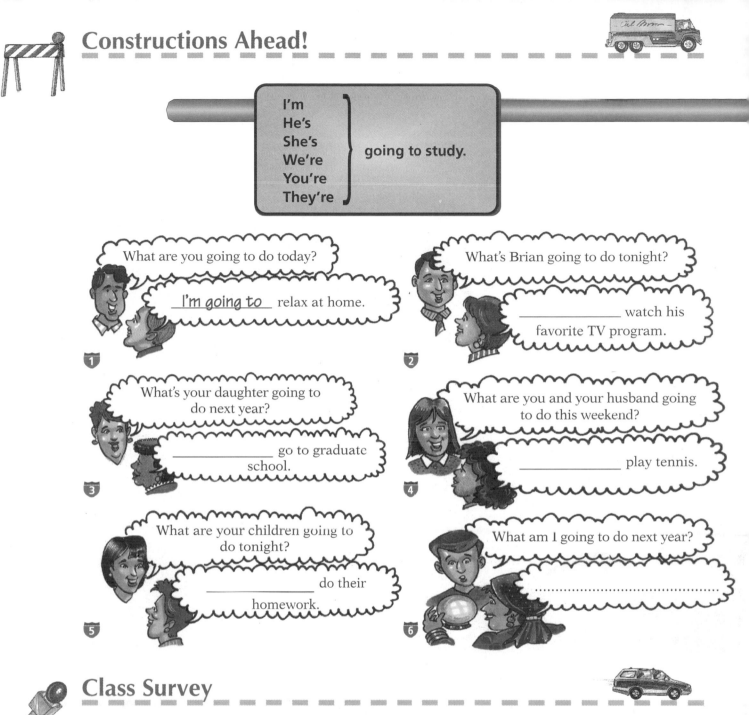

1. What are you going to do today?

___I'm going to___ relax at home.

2. What's Brian going to do tonight?

_____ watch his favorite TV program.

3. What's your daughter going to do next year?

_____ go to graduate school.

4. What are you and your husband going to do this weekend?

_____ play tennis.

5. What are your children going to do tonight?

_____ do their homework.

6. What am I going to do next year?

....

Class Survey

Take a survey of students in your class. Think of a question you would like to ask about the future. For example:

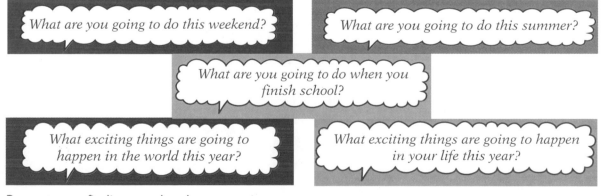

What are you going to do this weekend?

What are you going to do this summer?

What are you going to do when you finish school?

What exciting things are going to happen in the world this year?

What exciting things are going to happen in your life this year?

Report your findings to the class.

see a movie

It's raining.

A. What do you want to do today?

B. I don't know. What's the weather like?

A. It's raining. Do you want to see a movie?

B. Sure. That's a good idea.

go skiing

have a picnic

go to a museum

1 It's snowing.

2 It's sunny.

3 It's cloudy.

go swimming

stay home and watch TV

Make plans for today based on the weather.

4 It's hot.

5 It's cold.

The Weather

a. It's sunny.	c. It's raining	e. It's hot.
b. It's cloudy.	d. It's snowing.	f. It's cold.

1. ___b___   2. _____   3. _____

4. _____   5. _____   6. _____

Constructions Ahead!

I
We
You
They } want to see a movie.

He
She } wants to see a movie.

1. What do you want to do today?

2. What do your children want to do today?

3. What does Charles want to do today?

4. What does Sally want to do today?

5. What do you want to do tonight?

6. What do Bob and Karen want to do?

135

ExpressWays

a. see a movie   b. have a picnic   c. go skiing

1. *It's snowing. Do you want to __c__?*

2. *It's cloudy. Do you want to _____?*

3. *It's sunny. Do you want to _____?*

d. go swimming   e. stay home   f. take umbrellas

4. *It's raining. We should _____.*

5. *It's hot. We want to _____.*

6. *It's cold. I want to _____.*

g. go to the zoo   h. buy an umbrella   i. go to a museum

7. *It's cloudy. We should _____.*

8. *It's sunny. I'd like to _____.*

9. *It's raining. My husband wants to _____.*

InterView

It's sunny today. What should I do?

It's cloudy today. What should I do?

It's raining today. What should I do?

It's cold today. What should I do?

It's hot today. What should I do?

It's snowing today. What should I do?

Interview students in your class. Ask them for ideas of what to do in different kinds of weather. Then make a master list on the board of everybody's suggestions and see which are the most popular activities for each type of day.

136

More Weather

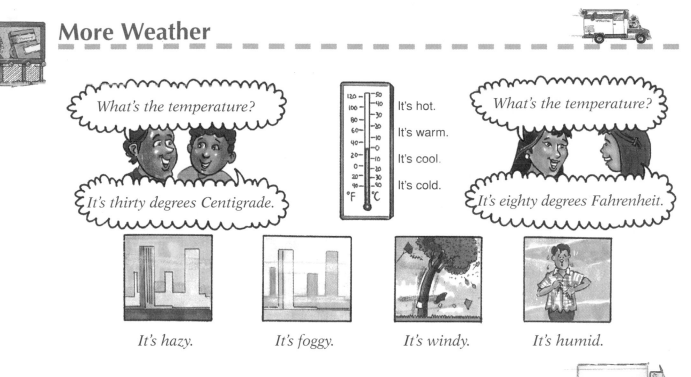

What's the temperature?

It's thirty degrees Centigrade.

It's hot.
It's warm.
It's cool.
It's cold.

What's the temperature?

It's eighty degrees Fahrenheit.

It's hazy.   *It's foggy.*   *It's windy.*   *It's humid.*

InterActions

You're a TV weather reporter! Report the weather around the world.

Hello. This is .... with the weather around the world today.

It's .... in .... The temperature there is .... It's a great day to ....!

It's .... in .... The temperature there is .... It's a great day to ....!

It's .... in .... The temperature there is .... It's a great day to ....!

And here in ...., it's .... The temperature here is .... It's a great day to ....!

This is .... reporting today's weather. Have a nice day!

REFLECTIONS
What are different ways to find out the weather forecast? Are weather forecasts very accurate in your area, or are they often wrong? Why?

Discuss in pairs or small groups, and then share your ideas with the class.

137

A. Do you want to go out for dinner tonight?

B. Tonight? I'm afraid I can't. I have to work late.

A. That's too bad.

B. Maybe we can go out for dinner some other time.

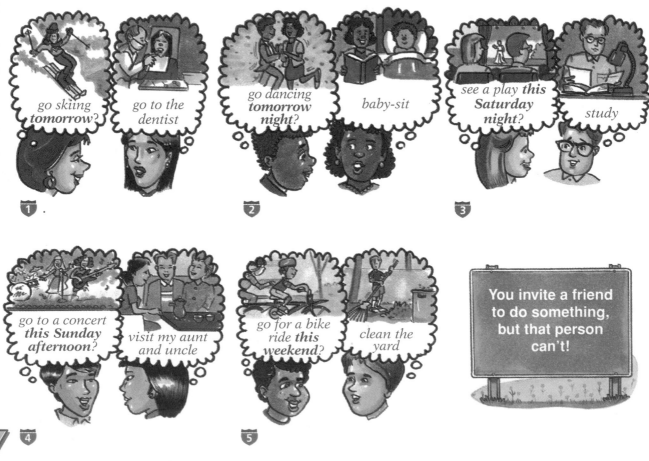

Constructions Ahead!

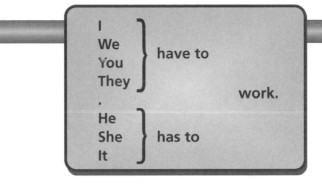

I		
We		
You	have to	
They		work.
.		
He		
She	has to	
It		

1. Can Tom go dancing tonight?

   No, _he can't_. _He has to_ baby-sit.

2. Can Maria see a play tonight?

   No, _____. _____ study for an exam.

3. Can your cousins come to the party?

   No, _____. _____ work this weekend.

4. Can you take me to the zoo tomorrow?

   No, _____. _____ type my term paper.

5. Can you and your wife come to dinner this Friday evening?

   No, _____. _____ go to a meeting.

InterActions

Helen doesn't want to go out with Norman. What do you think she's saying to him? Role-play the scene with another student.

Hi, Helen. This is Norman.

Oh hi, Norman.

I'm wondering, Helen. Do you want to go for a bike ride tomorrow morning?

I'm afraid I can't. ....

How about next weekend?

Gee, I'm sorry I can't. ....

Well, do you want to have dinner tomorrow?

I'm afraid I can't. ....

Do you want to have dinner with me next Monday?

I'm afraid I can't. ....

That's too bad. Maybe some other time.

Okay.

relax

relax–relaxed

A. Did you have a good weekend?

B. Yes, I did.

A. What did you do?

B. I relaxed.

play golf

play–played

A. Did you have a good weekend?

B. Yes, I did.

A. What did you do?

B. I played golf.

plant flowers

plant–planted

A. Did you have a good weekend?

B. Yes, I did.

A. What did you do?

B. I planted flowers.

write letters

write–wrote

A. Did you have a good weekend?

B. Yes, I did.

A. What did you do?

B. I wrote letters.

wash my car

1 wash–washed

clean my house

2 clean–cleaned

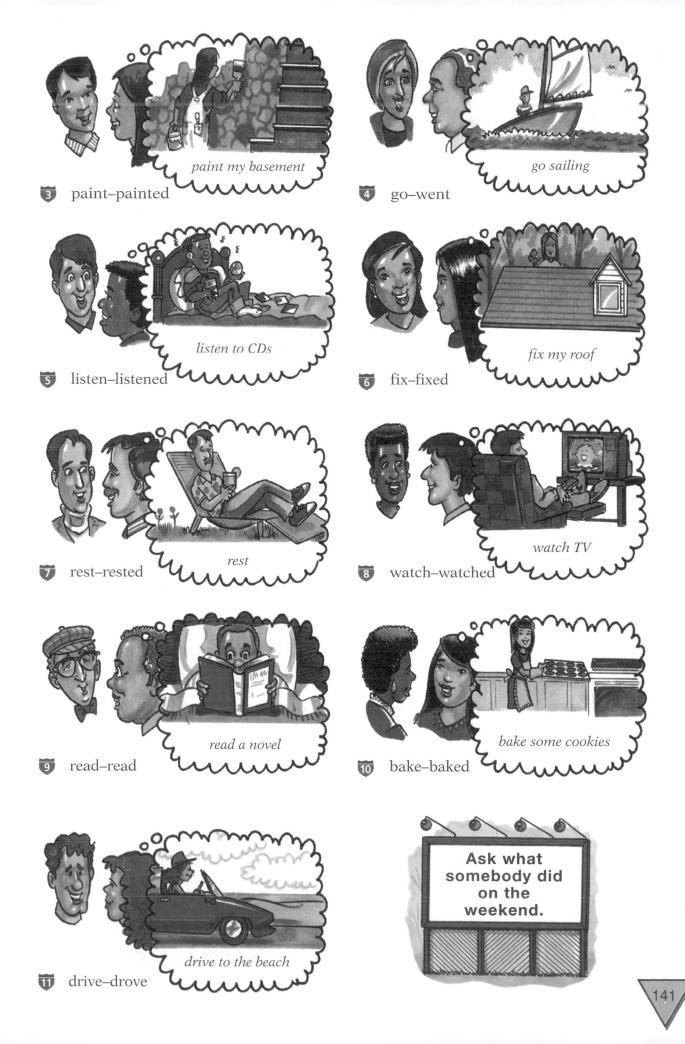

3 paint–painted
paint my basement

4 go–went
go sailing

5 listen–listened
listen to CDs

6 fix–fixed
fix my roof

7 rest–rested
rest

8 watch–watched
watch TV

9 read–read
read a novel

10 bake–baked
bake some cookies

11 drive–drove
drive to the beach

Ask what
somebody did
on the
weekend.

Constructions Ahead!

I
He
She
It } worked.
We
You
They

wash   plant   fix   write   read
watch   play   go   listen   clean

1 I _played_ tennis last weekend.

2 My husband _____ the dishes today.

3 Dorothy just _____ to the store.

4 My parents _____ TV last night.

5 Bill _____ his broken watch.

6 My daughter _____ her bedroom today.

7 I _____ a novel this weekend.

8 Sarah _____ flowers in the yard today.

9 I _____ letters to all my friends.

10 We _____ to the radio last night.

Listen

Listen and choose the correct answer.

1 a. yesterday
b. every day

2 a. yesterday
b. every day

3 a. yesterday
b. every day

4 a. yesterday
b. every day

5 a. yesterday
b. every day

6 a. yesterday
b. every day

7 a. yesterday
b. every day

8 a. yesterday
b. every day

9 a. yesterday
b. every day

Your Turn

For Writing and Discussion

Did you have a good weekend last weekend?
Tell all the things you did on the weekend.

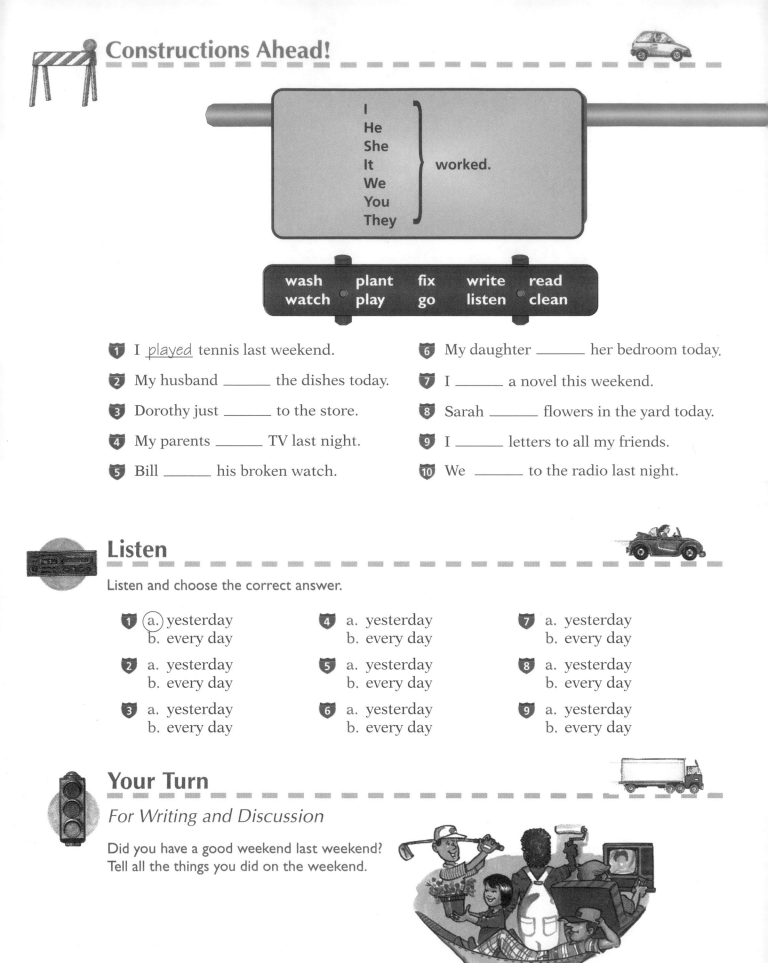

More Constructions Ahead!

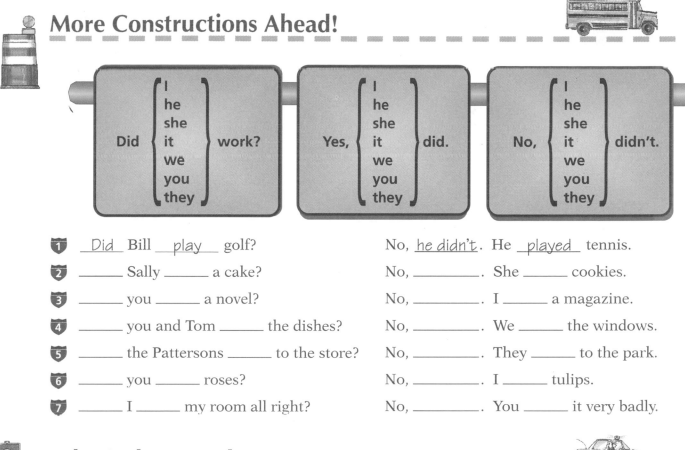

1. <u>Did</u> Bill <u>play</u> golf? — No, <u>he didn't</u>. He <u>played</u> tennis.
2. _____ Sally _____ a cake? — No, _____. She _____ cookies.
3. _____ you _____ a novel? — No, _____. I _____ a magazine.
4. _____ you and Tom _____ the dishes? — No, _____. We _____ the windows.
5. _____ the Pattersons _____ to the store? — No, _____. They _____ to the park.
6. _____ you _____ roses? — No, _____. I _____ tulips.
7. _____ I _____ my room all right? — No, _____. You _____ it very badly.

What's the Sound?

Say the words and put them in the correct column.

| cleaned | played | fixed | cooked | painted |
| listened | planted | watched | rested |

t	**d**	**ld**
fixed	cleaned	planted
_____	_____	_____
_____	_____	_____

Figure It Out!

Think of four things you did yesterday and have others in the class try to find out what you did by asking questions. For example:

Did you plant flowers?   *Did you watch TV?*   *Did you clean your house?*

Yes, I did.   *No, I didn't.*

play tennis   *go jogging*

play–played

A. Let's do something outdoors today.

B. All right. But I don't want to play tennis.
We played tennis last weekend.

A. Okay. What do you want to do?

B. I want to go jogging.

A. All right. That sounds like fun.

go swimming   *play basketball*   *have a picnic*   *go to the beach*   *take a walk in the park*   *play golf*

1 go–went   **2** have–had   **3** take–took

go sailing   *go to the zoo*   *drive to the mountains*   *go skating*   Make plans to do something outdoors today.

4 go–went   **5** drive–drove

144

ExpressWays

1. I really don't want to go to the beach today. <u>**I went to the beach**</u> last weekend.

2. We don't want to have a picnic today. _____ yesterday.

3. I don't want to play tennis now. _____ this morning.

4. I don't want to drive to the city tonight. _____ last night.

5. We don't want to go sailing. _____ last Sunday.

6. I don't want to play basketball now. _____ yesterday afternoon.

Listen

Listen and put the number next to the appropriate picture.

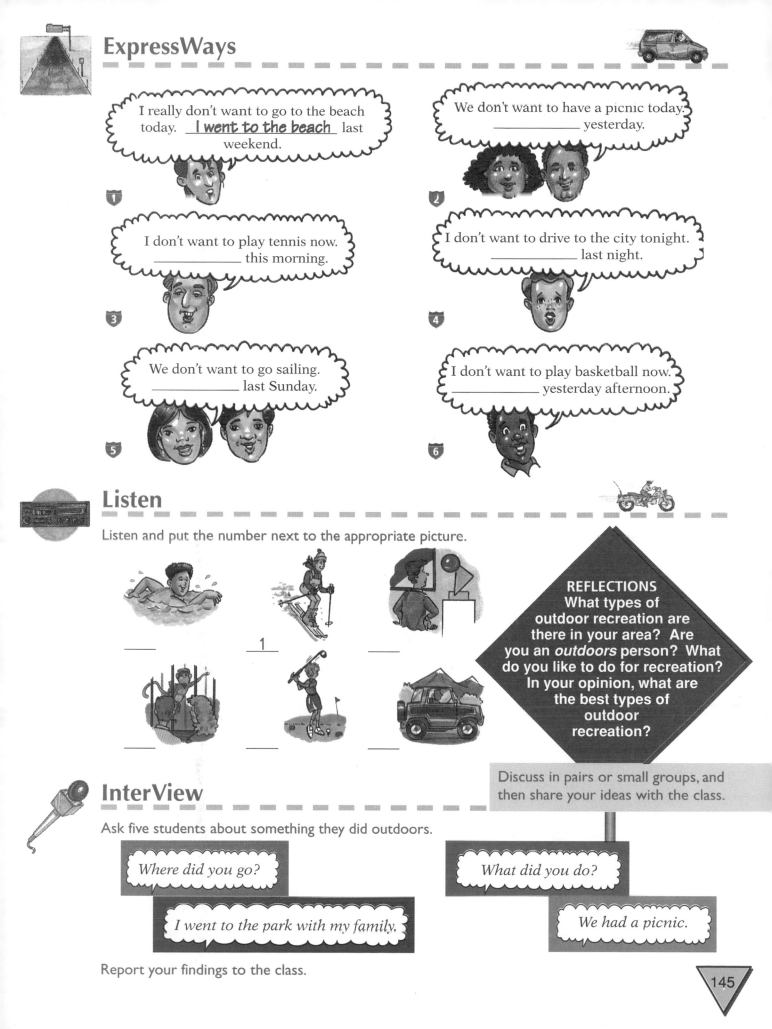

_____   1   _____

_____   _____   _____

REFLECTIONS
What types of outdoor recreation are there in your area? Are you an *outdoors* person? What do you like to do for recreation? In your opinion, what are the best types of outdoor recreation?

Discuss in pairs or small groups, and then share your ideas with the class.

InterView

Ask five students about something they did outdoors.

Where did you go?

I went to the park with my family.

What did you do?

We had a picnic.

Report your findings to the class.

at the movies

A. Where were you yesterday evening? I called you, but you weren't home.

B. That's right. I wasn't. I was at the movies.

A. Oh. What movie did you see?

B. I saw "Dancing in the Park."

A. Did you enjoy it?

B. Yes. It was excellent.

1 at the concert hall

2 at the theater

3 at the Greek restaurant

4 at the baseball stadium

5 at the county fair

You called a friend, but that person wasn't home.

* hear–heard

CrossTalk: *Movies*

Talk with a partner about the last movie you saw.

Who was in the movie?
What was the plot?
How was the movie? Was it good?
  bad? exciting? boring?
Do you recommend the movie?

Report to the class about your partner's movie.

CrossTalk: *Restaurants*

Talk with a partner about the last restaurant you went to.

What restaurant did you go to?
What did you order?
How was the service?
Do you recommend the restaurant?

Report to the class about your partner's restaurant.

CrossTalk: *Sporting Events*

Talk with a partner about the last sporting event you went to.

What was the sport?
How was the game?
What happened during the game?

Report to the class about your partner's sporting event.

Community Connections

Look in the newspaper and make a list of ten events that are happening this week in your city or town—movies, plays, concerts, sporting events. Bring the advertisements to class and tell which events you recommend going to ... and why.

Constructions Ahead!

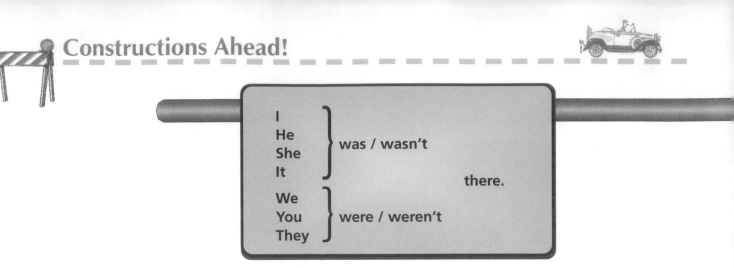

I
He
She
It
} was / wasn't

We
You
They
} were / weren't

there.

1 ___Were___ you home last night?   Yes. I ___was___ there all night.

2 _____ your children home last night?   Yes, they _____. We _____ all home last night.

3 The weather _____ very good today.   I know. It rained all day. It _____ a very bad day.

4 Where _____ you yesterday? You _____ at work.   I know. I _____ at home. I _____ sick in bed all day.

5 How _____ the party last night?   It _____ terrible. The food _____ very good, and the music _____ awful, too!

What's the Answer?

It ((was) wasn't)[1] Janet's birthday last night. She wanted to do something special. She called her friends Melissa and Jane, but they (wasn't weren't)[2] home. She wanted to talk to her friend Carlos, but he (was wasn't)[3] home. She called her sister Debbie, but she (was were)[4] out somewhere. Janet couldn't even find her dog Sparky. He (was wasn't)[5] outdoors somewhere.

She went to her Aunt Sally and Uncle Charlie's house. They (wasn't weren't)[6] home. Then she went to visit her grandmother and grandfather. She (was were)[7] sure they (was were)[8] home. Janet (was were)[9] right! They (were weren't)[10] home! And surprise!! Everybody else was at their house, too. Melissa and Jane (was were)[11] there. Carlos, Debbie, and her other friends (was were)[12] there. And of course her parents and grandparents (was were)[13] there. Even her dog Sparky (was wasn't)[14] there. It (was were)[15] a wonderful party!

148

Reading: *Howie Just Wanted to Have Fun!*

Howie Henderson is a college student in New York City. Last weekend he was supposed to study for an exam, but he didn't really want to study. He just wanted to have fun. On Friday night he went dancing. On Saturday morning he played tennis with his friend Keith. On Saturday afternoon his friends called, and they all had a picnic together in Central Park. On Saturday evening he went to a party at his friend Roger's apartment. He went to bed at about midnight.

On Sunday the weather was bad. It was cold and cloudy. It was a good day to study, but Howie didn't want to. Instead he went to see a movie. The title of the film was *Cloudy Monday*. Howie didn't like it at all. It was a comedy, and Howie doesn't like comedies very much.

Finally on Sunday night, Howie studied for the exam. He studied from six in the evening until two in the morning. On Monday morning Howie went to school and took the exam. He was tired, and he wasn't at all prepared. Naturally, he did very badly on the exam.

Howie was sorry he didn't study for the test. He just wanted to have fun!

Yes, No, or Maybe?

1. Howie Henderson goes to college.
2. Last weekend he wanted to study.
3. He didn't study on Friday night.
4. He called his friend Keith to play tennis on Saturday morning.
5. He and his friends had a picnic on Saturday afternoon.
6. There were a lot of people at his friend Roger's party.
7. Sunday's weather wasn't good.
8. Howie's friends invited him to see a movie.
9. Howie didn't like the movie.
10. Howie studied for three hours on Sunday evening.
11. Howie did well on the exam.
12. Howie is a serious student.

Your Turn

For Writing and Discussion

Tell about a time you "had fun"! Where did you go? What did you do? Who were you with? (Hopefully, you didn't have an exam you were supposed to study for!)

What Do You Like to Do?

A. What do you like to do for exercise?

B. I like to do yoga. How about you?

A. I like to swim.

B. That's interesting. Did you swim today?

A. Yes, I did. I swam this morning. How about you? Did you do yoga today?

B. Yes, I did. I did yoga after work.

A. Oh. That's interesting.

A. What do you like to do for exercise?

B. I like to _____. How about you?

A. I like to _____.

B. That's interesting. Did you _____ today?

A. Yes, I did. I _____ this morning. How about you?
Did you _____ today?

B. Yes, I did. I _____ after work.

A. Oh. That's interesting.

You're talking with a new friend about your exercise routine. Create an original conversation, using the model dialog above as a guide. Feel free to adapt and expand the model any way you wish.

Constructions Ahead!

> | I
We
You
They } like to swim. | He
She } likes to swim. |

1. I like to bake cakes and cookies. My husband _____likes to_____ bake bread.

2. I _____ swim at the beach. My wife _____ swim at the lake.

3. Our children _____ do their homework right after dinner.

4. I don't _____ play tennis. I _____ play golf. My husband doesn't _____ play golf. He _____ play tennis. We're very different.

5. All the people in our family _____ read. My brother _____ read adventure stories. My sister _____ read biographies. I _____ read science fiction stories. And my parents _____ read novels.

CrossTalk

Make a list of five things you like to do and five things you don't like to do.

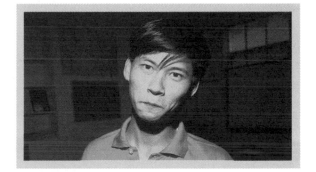

I like to …	I don't like to …
....	....
....	....
....	....
....	....
....	....

Talk with a partner and compare your likes and dislikes. Report your findings to the class.

Looking Back

☐ **Recreation and Entertainment**
baseball stadium
beach
bike ride
concert
concert hall
county fair
dancing
dinner
garden
mountains
movie (the movies)
museum

park
party
picnic
play
restaurant
theater
TV
walk
zoo

☐ **Weather**
cloudy
cold
foggy

hazy
hot
humid
raining
snowing
sunny
windy

☐ **Sports**
baseball
basketball
golf
jogging
sailing

skating
skiing
swimming
tennis

☐ **Everyday Activities**
bake
clean
drive
fix
paint
plant
play
read

relax
rest
study
visit
wash
write

Now Leaving Exit 8 Construction Area

☐ **Future: Going to**
☐ **Like to**
☐ **Have to**
☐ **Want to**
☐ **Time Expressions**
☐ **Past Tense**
☐ **Irregular Verbs**

Sorry for the inconvenience. For more information see pages 164–165.

ExpressWays Checklist

I can . . .

☐ tell about weekend plans
☐ tell about weather
☐ make plans for the day
☐ make and respond to invitations
☐ tell about weekend activities
☐ share information about the past
☐ tell about things I like to do

REST STOP

Take a break!
Have a conversation!

Here are some scenes from Exits 7 and 8.

Who do you think these people are?
What do you think they're talking about?

In pairs or small groups, create conversations based on these scenes and act them out.

Appendix

- **Grammar Constructions**
- **Cardinal Numbers**
- **Ordinal Numbers**
- **Irregular Verbs**
- **Tape Scripts for Listening Exercises**
- **Topic Index**
- **Grammar Index**

Exit 1 Constructions

To Be
Subject Pronouns

(I am)	I'm
(he is)	he's
(she is)	she's
(we are)	we're
(you are)	you're
(they are)	they're

Possessive Adjectives

I	my
he	his
she	her
we	our
you	your
they	their

WH-Questions

What's your name?
Where are you from?

To Be: Yes/No Questions

Are you from Tokyo?
   Yes, I am.

Exit 2 Constructions

To Be: Yes/No Questions

Am	I	
Is	he she it	here?
Are	we you they	

To Be: Negatives

	I'm	not.
No,	he she it	isn't.
	we you they	aren't.

Present Continuous Tense

(I am)	I'm	
(He is)	He's	
(She is)	She's	
(It is)	It's	working.
(We are)	We're	
(You are)	You're	
(They are)	They're	

WH-Questions

What are you doing?
Where are you going?
How do you spell that?

Present Continuous Tense
Possessive Adjectives

(I am)	I'm		my	
(He is)	He's		his	
(She is)	She's	cleaning	her	room.
(We are)	We're		our	
(You are)	You're		your	
(They are)	They're		their	

Exit 3 Constructions

There Is

Is there a post office nearby?

There's a post office on Main Street.

Yes, **there is**.
No, **there isn't**.

Prepositions of Location

It's **on** Main Street.
It's **next to** the bank.
It's **across from** the bus station.
It's **between** the library and
the clinic.
It's **around the corner from** the
movie theater.

Simple Present Tense

Does this bus go to Westville?
No, it **doesn't**.

It **goes** to Riverside.

Simple Present Tense vs. To Be

Is this Bus Number 42?
Yes, it **is**.
No, it **isn't**.

Does this bus stop at Center Street?
Yes, it **does**.
No, it **doesn't**.

Short Answers

Yes, it is.
No, it isn't.

Yes, it docs.
No, it doesn't.

Imperatives

Walk that way to Second Avenue.
Take the Second Avenue bus and
get off at Park Street.

WH-Questions

Which bus goes to Westville?

Exit 4 Constructions

Singular/Plural

It has one bedroom.
It has two bedrooms.

There's a nice refrigerator.
There are four windows.

Articles: A, An, The

A cookie	**An** apple
A tomato	**An** egg
A banana	**An** orange

Where are **the** carrots?
Where's **the** butter?

Count Nouns

| There aren't any more | carrots.
tomatoes.
apples. |
| Where are the | carrots?
potatoes?
peaches? |

Non-Count Nouns

| There isn't any more | milk.
bread.
cheese. |
| Where's the | butter?
sugar?
rice? |

This/That/These/Those

Where do you want **this** sofa?
That sofa?

How about **these** chairs?
Those chairs?

Imperatives

Put it in the living room.
Please put them in the dining room.

Simple Present Tense vs. To Be

How much **is** the rent?

Do you want to see the apartment?
Does that include utilities?

Have/Has

I **have** an apartment for you.
It **has** two bedrooms.

Some/Any

I'll get **some** more.

There aren't **any** more cookies.

Exit 5 Constructions

Simple Present Tense

What do	I we you they	do?	I We You They	work.
What does	he she it	do?	He She It	works.

Simple Present Tense: s vs. non-s Endings

I We You They	work. sell. fix.	
He She It	works. sells. fixes.	[s] [z] [ɪz]

Object Pronouns

I	me
he	him
she	her
it	it
we	us
you	you
they	them

Adverbs of Frequency

100%	always
↑	usually
	often
	sometimes
↓	rarely
0%	never

Can

I He She It We You They	can/can't	work.	Can you work? Yes, I can. No, I can't.

Exit 6 Constructions

Imperatives

Touch your toes.
Be sure to follow the directions.

Should

I He She It We You They	should	stop.

Simple Present Tense vs. To Be

Do you smoke?
   No, I **don't**.

Are you allergic?
   No, **I'm not**.

Short Answers

No, I don't.
No, I'm not.

No, there isn't.

Have/Has

I We You They	have	a headache.
He She	has	

Time Expressions

1:00	one o'clock
1:15	one fifteen
1:30	one thirty
1:45	one forty-five

this morning
this afternoon
tomorrow morning
tomorrow afternoon
this Friday
next Friday

tomorrow morning **at** 9:00

three **times a day**
twice a day
before each meal
after each meal

Possessive Nouns

Doctor's Office.
Sally Wilson's son.

Count Nouns

Where can I find **them**?
They're in Aisle 3.

Non-Count Nouns

Where can I find **it**?
It's in Aisle 2.

Exit 7 Constructions

Singular/Plural

[s] I'm looking for **a shirt**.
Shirts are in Aisle 3.

[z] I'm looking for **a tie**.
Ties are in Aisle 3.

[ɪz] I'm looking for **a dress**.
Dresses are in Aisle 3.

I'm looking for	a	shirt. tie. dress.
	a pair of	pants shoes. pajamas.

Prepositions of Location

in Aisle 3
on that counter
in the back of the store
in the front of the store
near the elevator
over there

Adjectives

a **size 36 black** belt
a **medium green** sweater
a **small brown** raincoat

Too + Adjective

It's **too** short.
They're **too** long.

WH-Questions

What size do you want?
Where are the rest rooms?
How does the jacket fit?
How many postal workers are there?
How much does it cost?

Exit 8 Constructions

Future: Going to

What	am	I	going to do?	(I am)	I'm	going to read.
	is	he she it		(He is) (She is) (It is)	He's She's It's	
	are	we you they		(We are) (You are) (They are)	We're You're They're	

Have to

I We You They	have to	work.
He She It	has to	

Like to

I We You They	like to	work.
He She It	likes to	

Want to

I We You They	want to	work.
He She It	wants to	

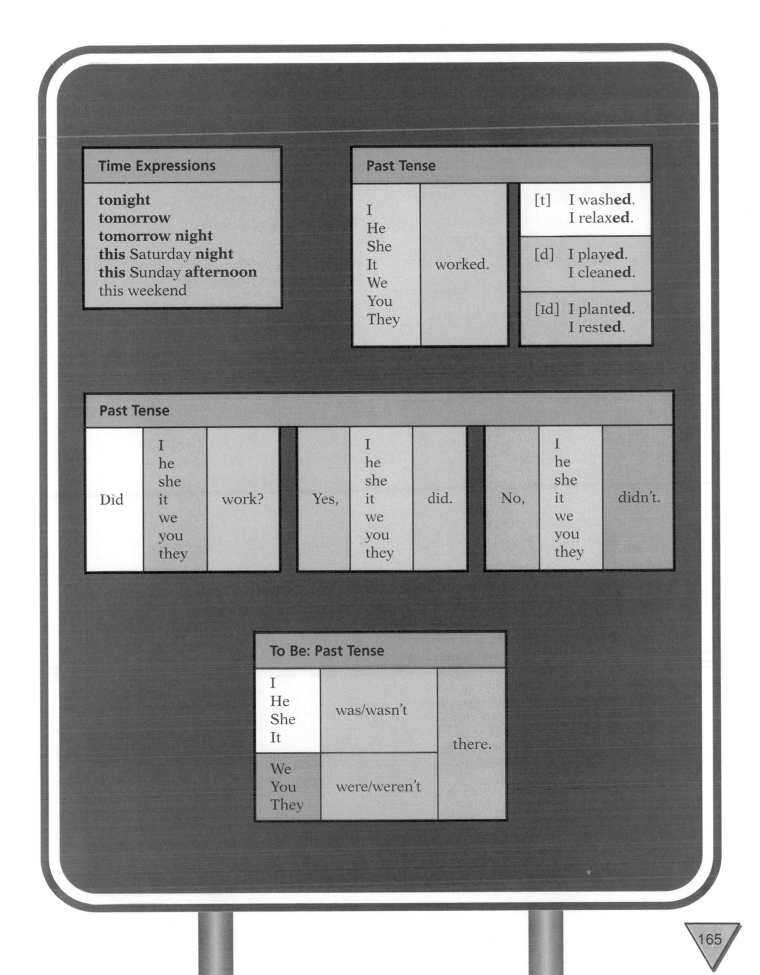

Time Expressions

tonight
tomorrow
tomorrow night
this Saturday **night**
this Sunday **afternoon**
this weekend

Past Tense

I He She It We You They	worked.	[t]	I wash**ed**. I relax**ed**.
		[d]	I play**ed**. I clean**ed**.
		[Id]	I plant**ed**. I rest**ed**.

Past Tense

Did	I he she it we you they	work?	Yes,	I he she it we you they	did.	No,	I he she it we you they	didn't.

To Be: Past Tense

I He She It	was/wasn't	there.
We You They	were/weren't	

CARDINAL NUMBERS

1	one	20	twenty	
2	two	21	twenty-one	
3	three	22	twenty-two	
4	four	.		
5	five	.		
6	six	29	twenty-nine	
7	seven	30	thirty	
8	eight	40	forty	
9	nine	50	fifty	
10	ten	60	sixty	
11	eleven	70	seventy	
12	twelve	80	eighty	
13	thirteen	90	ninety	
14	fourteen	100	one hundred	
15	fifteen	200	two hundred	
16	sixteen	300	three hundred	
17	seventeen	.		
18	eighteen	.		
19	nineteen	900	nine hundred	
		1,000	one thousand	
		2,000	two thousand	
		3,000	three thousand	
		.		
		.		
		10,000	ten thousand	
		100,000	one hundred thousand	
		1,000,000	one million	

ORDINAL NUMBERS

1st	first	20th	twentieth
2nd	second	21st	twenty-first
3rd	third	22nd	twenty-second
4th	fourth		.
5th	fifth		.
6th	sixth	29th	twenty-ninth
7th	seventh	30th	thirtieth
8th	eighth	40th	fortieth
9th	ninth	50th	fiftieth
10th	tenth	60th	sixtieth
11th	eleventh	70th	seventieth
12th	twelfth	80th	eightieth
13th	thirteenth	90th	ninetieth
14th	fourteenth	100th	one hundredth
15th	fifteenth		
16th	sixteenth	1,000th	one thousandth
17th	seventeenth	1,000,000th	one millionth
18th	eighteenth		
19th	nineteenth		

IRREGULAR VERBS

be	was
do	did
drive	drove
go	went
have	had
hear	heard
read	read
see	saw
take	took
write	wrote

Page 7

Listen 1

Listen and write the missing letters.

1. B-R-E-N-N-E-R
2. B-A-R-B-A-R-A
3. C-L-A-Y-T-O-N
4. S-M-I-T-H
5. K-W-A-N
6. K-E-L-T-O-N
7. P-E-T-E-R-S-O-N
8. M-I-C-H-A-E-L
9. H-U-S-B-A-N-D
10. J-E-S-S-I-C-A

Listen 2

Listen and choose the right answer.

1. Could you spell that, please?
2. What's your first name?
3. What's your name?
4. And your last name?
5. What's your first name?
6. Could you spell that, please?

Page 9

Listen 1

Listen and write the number of the address you hear.

1. A. What's your address?
   B. 6 Maple Street.

2. A. What's your address?
   B. 11 Pond Avenue.

3. A. What's your address?
   B. 14 Howard Street.

4. A. What's your address?
   B. 3 Main Street.

5. A. What's your address?
   B. 17 Summer Street.

6. A. What's your address?
   B. 1812 Central Avenue.

Listen 2

Listen and write the missing numbers.

1. A. What's your telephone number?
   B. 543-6905.

2. A. What's your telephone number?
   B. 249-1986.

3. A. What's your telephone number?
   B. 673-5220.

4. A. What's your telephone number?
   B. 946-1682.

5. A. What's your telephone number?
   B. 892-0677.

6. A. What's your telephone number?
   B. 439-1708.

Listen 3

Listen and choose the right answer.

1. What's your address?
2. What's your telephone number?
3. What's your name?
4. What's your address?
5. What's your phone number?
6. What's your last name?

Page 13

Listen and choose the best answer.

1. Where are you from?
2. Are you Australian?
3. Are you from New York?
4. What's your phone number?
5. What's your first name?
6. Are you Mrs. Watanabe?

Page 19

Listen 1

Listen and choose the answer to the question you hear.

1. Is this 547-2055?
2. Is this 498-5930?
3. Is this 622-6835?
4. Is this 356-9472?
5. Is this 285-2841?
6. Is this 771-9562?

Listen 2

Listen and write the missing numbers.

1. A. I'd like the number of Donald Jenkins.
   B. Just a moment . . . the number is 573-5108.

2. A. What's the telephone number, please?
   B. 963-6882.

3. A. I'd like your telephone number.
   B. My number is 527-5382.

4. A. What's your telephone number?
   B. 623-4406.

5. A. And what's your telephone number, please?
   B. My number is 572-4329.

6. A. I'd like the number of Peter Graves.
   B. Just a moment . . . the number is 248-9206.

Page 29

Listen to the conversation and choose the correct picture.

1. A. What's Jeff doing?
   B. He's cooking dinner.

2. A. What are Mr. and Mrs. Parker doing?
   B. They're going to the mall.

3. A. What are you doing?
   B. We're doing our homework.

4. A. What are your children doing?
   B. They're brushing their teeth.

5. A. Where is Mrs. Lee going?
   B. She's going to the library.

6. A. What's your husband doing?
   B. He's eating dinner.

7. A. What's Jane doing?
   B. She's looking for her car.

8. A. Are you busy?
   B. Yes. I'm washing the dishes.

9. A. What are Kathy and Bob doing?
   B. They're dancing.

10. A. What's your son doing?
    B. He's doing his exercises.

Page 38

Listen and choose the correct place.

1. It's on Main Street, next to the bank.
2. It's on Central Avenue, across from the clinic.
3. It's on Central Avenue, around the corner from the hotel.
4. It's on Central Avenue, next to the grocery store.
5. It's on Jefferson Boulevard, across from the mall.
6. It's on Central Avenue, across from the bus station.
7. It's on Appleton Boulevard, around the corner from the laundromat.
8. It's on Central Avenue, next to the gas station and across from the movie theater.
9. It's on Main Street, around the corner from the supermarket.
10. It's on Appleton Boulevard, across from the zoo.
11. It's on Appleton Boulevard, around the corner from the hotel.
12. It's on Central Avenue, next to the gas station and across from the police station.

Page 41

Listen to each conversation. What number do you hear?

1. A. Which bus goes downtown?
   B. Bus Number 29.

2. A. Which train goes to Waterbury?
   B. Number 43.

3. A. Does this bus go to the park?
   B. No, take Bus Number 35.

4. A. Does this bus go to New Haven?
   B. No, take Number 20.

5. A. What's your address?
   B. 68 Central Avenue.

6. A. Which bus goes to the beach?
   B. Take Bus Number 72.

7. A. What's your address?
   B. It's 58 Grand Avenue.

8. A. What's your address?
   B. It's 4936 Michigan Avenue.

9. A. Is there a post office nearby?
   B. Yes. There's a post office at 4560 Riverdale Avenue.

Page 43

Listen to each question and choose the correct answer.

1. Does this plane go to Bankok?
2. Does this train stop at City Hospital?
3. Is this the Number 4 bus?
4. Is this 429-9292?
5. Does this bus go to Phoenix?
6. Is this the downtown train?
7. Does this bus stop at the shopping mall?
8. Does this train go to downtown Seoul?

Page 49

Listen to the conversations and choose the correct answer.

1. A. Take Bus Number 25 to Summer Street.
   B. Sorry. Did you say Bus Number 23?

2. A. Walk that way two blocks.
   B. Sorry. Did you say two blocks?

3. A. Drive that way twelve miles.
   B. Did you say twelve miles?

4. A. Turn left on Third Street.
   B. I'm sorry. Did you say Fifth Street?

5. A. Go five blocks and turn right.
   B. Did you say five blocks?

6. A. Turn right on Crosstown Boulevard and go seven blocks.
   B. Did you say eleven blocks?

7. A. Take the Fourth Street bus and get off at Broad Street.
   B. Sorry. Did you say the First Street bus?

8. A. Take the Expressway and get off at Exit 24.
   B. Did you say Exit 24?

9. A. The post office is at forty-two twenty-two Harrison Avenue.
   B. Forty-two twenty-two?

10. A. My telephone number is 276-1274.
    B. Sorry. Did you say 276-1264?

Page 57

Listen and choose the word you hear.

1. The apartment has a very nice bathroom.
2. I'm looking for a two-bedroom apartment.
3. What a nice balcony!
4. This apartment has a large bedroom and a very nice dining room.
5. I'm looking for an apartment downtown.
6. This apartment has only one bedroom, but it has two bathrooms.

Page 59

Someone is calling you about this apartment. Answer the person's questions based on this diagram of the apartment.

1. I'm calling about the apartment for rent. Tell me, is there a shower in the bathroom?
2. Is there a fireplace in the living room?
3. How many bedrooms are there in the apartment?
4. And I was wondering . . . Is there a closet in the living room?
5. And tell me about the kitchen. Is there a refrigerator in the kitchen?
6. How about a stove? Is there a stove in the kitchen?

Page 61

Listen 1

Which apartment is being described?

1. The rent is four hundred and thirty dollars.
2. The rent is two hundred and twenty-five dollars.
3. I have a three-bedroom apartment for you. The rent is five hundred and eighty dollars.
4. The rent is six hundred and fifty dollars plus utilities.
5. I have a very nice apartment for you. It has two bedrooms.

Listen 2

What number do you hear?

1. A. How much is the rent?
   B. It's six hundred dollars a month.

2. A. How much is the gas?
   B. About fifty dollars a month.

3. A. About how much is the electricity?
   B. Hmm. About sixty dollars a month.

4. A. And how many parking spaces are there?
   B. Hmm. Let's see. I think there are fifty.

5. A. What's the parking fee?
   B. It's one hundred dollars a month.

6. A. What's the address?
   B. Twenty-nine thirty-seven Broad Street.

Page 65

Listen 1

Listen and choose the correct picture.

1. A. Where do you want this table?
   B. Put it in the kitchen.

2. A. I'm afraid there aren't any more bananas.
   B. There aren't?

3. A. What are you looking for?
   B. The plants.

4. A. I'm looking for a lamp.
   B. This lamp?

5. A. Where do you want these pictures?
   B. Put them in the living room.

6. A. What are you looking for?
   B. An egg.

Listen 2

Which word do you hear?

1. There aren't any more tomatoes.
2. Is there a refrigerator in the kitchen?
3. Are there any eggs in the refrigerator?
4. I'm looking for a cookie.
5. I'll get some more bananas when I go to the supermarket.

6. Do you want to see the neighborhood?
7. I'm afraid there aren't any more oranges.
8. There aren't any more chairs.
9. There are two elevators in the building.

Page 69

What numbers and letters do you hear?

1. I'm sorry. Did you say eight?
2. The rice is in Aisle B.
3. It's in Aisle M.
4. Sorry. Did you say G?
5. Is there butter in Aisle 3?
6. There are nine potatoes in the refrigerator.
7. The carrots? They're in Aisle A.
8. I'm looking for Aisle 10C.
9. I'm sorry. Did you say eighteen?

Page 77

Listen and choose the correct answer.

1. Jack is a mechanic. He . . .
2. Ruth is a salesperson. She . . .
3. I'm a teacher. I . . .
4. My son is an assembler. He . . .
5. Barbara is a bilingual secretary. She . . .
6. My wife and I are writers. We . . .
7. I'm a delivery person. I . . .
8. Jane is an architect. She . . .

Page 93

Listen and write the number under the correct picture.

1. I have a headache.
2. Sam has a stomachache.
3. I'm sorry to hear that Charles has an earache.
4. Nancy has a sore throat today.
5. Rita has a backache.
6. Jim has a toothache.

Page 97

What time can the doctor see these people?

1. Can you come in at ten fifteen?
2. Can you come in today at five o'clock?
3. Can you come in tomorrow at three forty-five?

4. Can you come in tomorrow morning at six thirty?
5. Can you come in tomorrow at nine fifteen?
6. Can you come in tomorrow afternoon at four forty-five?
7. Can you come in Thursday morning at eleven?
8. Can you come in Tuesday afternoon at one thirty?

Page 99

Listen to the conversation and answer these questions.

A. I have just a few more questions. Do you smoke?
B. No, I don't.
A. And are you allergic to anything?
B. Yes. I'm allergic to penicillin.
A I see. Do you have other allergies?
B. No. I'm allergic only to penicillin.
A. Do you drink alcohol?
B. No, I never drink alcohol.
A. And do you exercise regularly?
B. Yes. I exercise every day.
A. Tell me, is there a history of heart disease in your family?
B. No, there isn't.
A. Finally, are you currently having any medical problems?
B. Yes. I have a bad stomachache.
A. Are you taking anything for it?
B. Yes. I'm taking Tummy-Aid Tablets.
A. Tummy-Aid Tablets?
B. Yes.
A. Okay. I think that's all the information I need. The doctor will see you shortly.

Page 105

Listen to the directions and choose the appropriate medicine bottle.

1. Take one pill four times a day.
2. Take three tablets twice a day.
3. Be sure to take one capsule three times a day.
4. Follow the directions. Take one teaspoon twice a day.

5. Be sure to follow the directions. Take two capsules two times a day.
6. Be sure to follow the directions on the label. Take one pill once a day.

Page 115

What article of clothing do you hear?

1. I'm looking for a sweater.
2. Ties are over there.
3. I'm looking for a long-sleeved shirt.
4. Dresses are in the front of the store.
5. I have some nice blouses for you.
6. Here you are ... two black belts.
7. There's a brown coat over there.
8. Raincoats are on that rack.
9. I'm looking for two or three pairs of socks.

Page 117

Listen and choose the appropriate picture.

1. This jacket is too short.
2. This skirt is too large.
3. I think that suit is too small.
4. These sneakers are too tight.
5. I think these gloves are too big.
6. I think these pants are too long.

Page 119

What number do you hear?

1. Men's Clothing is on the first floor.
2. You can eat lunch on the ninth floor.
3. Women's Clothing is on the seventh floor.
4. Children's Clothing is on the fifth floor.
5. Restrooms are on the eighth floor.
6. TVs and radios are on the fourth floor.
7. Bedroom furniture is on the third floor.
8. The Customer Service Counter is on the seventh floor.
9. Belts and ties are on the first floor.

What amount do you hear?

1. That's eleven dollars and fifteen cents.
2. That comes to sixty-four dollars and thirty cents.
3. That's forty-three fifty.
4. With the tax, that comes to seventy-eight sixty-four.
5. That comes to one hundred and thirty-eight dollars and forty-three cents, and that includes tax.
6. That comes to two hundred and seventy-nine dollars and sixty-three cents.

Listen and choose the appropriate picture.

1. I want to buy some aerogrammes.
2. I'd like some stamps, please.
3. I want to send a registered letter.
4. I'd like to mail a package to Japan.
5. Where can I buy a money order?
6. Where do I file this change of address form?

Listen and choose the correct response.

1. Where's this package going?
2. How do you want to send this letter?
3. Is this package valuable?
4. Do you want to insure this letter?
5. Can you help me?
6. Where can I buy stamps?
7. Are these letters going to Miami?
8. How do you want to send this package?

Listen and choose the correct answer.

1. I baked a cake.
2. I write letters.
3. My husband fixed our roof.
4. Margaret watches the news on TV after dinner.

5. We rested all day.
6. The Petersons drive their children to school.
7. I go to work.
8. My wife and I went to a concert.
9. I wrote a letter.

Listen and put the number next to the apporiate picture.

1. I went skiing last weekend.
2. Mr. and Mrs. Benson went to the zoo yesterday.
3. Martha played golf this morning.
4. Jerry went swimming this afternoon.
5. I went to a museum this weekend.
6. Yesterday morning I drove to the mountains.

GRAMMAR INDEX

TOPIC INDEX